START UGLY

THE UNEXPECTED PATH TO EVERYDAY CREATIVITY

DAVID DUCHEMIN

CRAFT & VISION

START UGLY

THE UNEXPECTED PATH TO EVERYDAY CREATIVITY

David duChemin
www.davidduchemin.com

Editor: Cynthia Haynes
Project Manager: Corwin Hiebert
Proofreader: Kate Siobhan Mulligan

Cover Image: *The Ugly Duchess*, Quentin Matsys, c.1513, Public Domain

ISBN 978-0-9917557-9-0
First Edition, July 2020
© 2020 David duChemin

Published by Craft & Vision
A Division of Pixelated Image Communications, Inc
CraftAndVision.com

Printed in the USA

TO
EVERYONE
WHO
HAS
EVER
HAD
THE
ASTONISHING
COURAGE
TO
START
UGLY
ON
THEIR
WAY
TO
SOMETHING
MORE,
AND
TO
THOSE
ABOUT
TO.

CONTENTS

CONTENTS

01
THE UGLY PROBLEM

The fact that it took me a couple of months longer than I expected to begin a book about *starting* feels like it should be an omen to me. Perhaps I should write a book about irony instead. The coffee cup beside me says "Create" in bold, mocking font, like it's taunting me.

And still I begin. Look at me go. I'm already 62 words in. I should reward myself. Maybe go downstairs and get a bagel, though I'm out of cream cheese so I should probably head to the store. So much for writing. Dammit. This isn't going well.

But it *is* going well. I know this because I've started the hardest work of any single thing we do or make: *beginning*. It has been this way with every book I've written (this is my 31st, if you count my eBooks), every article, every series of photographs, every project around the house. Going back over a decade to a time in my life when I made a career as a comedian it was most certainly the case; getting on stage and starting was always the hardest part.

Beginnings are hard. They always have been and always will be, but after 25 years of making my living solely on the results of my creative efforts, I've come to accept that they—the beginnings—are the most important part of the creative process. At least they are for me, and this seems to be true of my students as well, among whom the most common frustration I hear is some version of, "I just don't know where to begin," or, "I just can't get started."

To be sure, there are frustrations aplenty in the creative life. The creative process is not a paint-by-number kit; it comes with no guarantees. There are people who, once started, also get stalled in the messy middle of a project, and others who just never quite finish. These are problems of their own. But they're problems we'll never have the joy of solving unless we take the first hesitant steps and just begin.

I'd also like to suggest that there is no one and only Start to every project, but many. You start when you sit down to begin a thing and plan it out. You start when you begin, in the case of a book, to write the ninth chapter even when you're not sure where it's going, and you start a new phase when you write the final words, or wrap production on the album or movie and ship the work you've created. Every day is a new start.

The basic premise of this book is that starting any creative effort is the most important step and doesn't have to be so paralyzing. Much of the difficulty is related to fear, but also to a misunderstanding of the creative process itself and a lack of reliable tools to help pry things loose in that process.

Underlying that is another premise and that's the fundamental notion that creativity is not reserved only for the arts. Writers, sculptors, painters, dancers, photographers, and anyone who readily identifies with being a "creative" will immediately know the challenge of the process. Some of us take a certain pleasure in how difficult it can be. But we are not the only ones who create, or make.

Creativity is not reserved for the exclusive use of those who imagine themselves in touch with the muses. It's the right and privilege of every human being. It is what separates us–for good or for bad–from the rest of the animals with whom we share the planet. We make, not just because we must, as birds do to make a nest or as beavers do to build their dams, but because we can. Because it brings us joy and challenges us and gives us meaning, and yes, in some cases also because we must. We must because we need homes and cures for diseases, but also because there is some inner force that won't go away until we silence it with the making.

Here's what is incredible about the process of making, and the way our brains work: I sat down half an hour ago with the intention of scribbling some words that I hoped would make the introduction to this book. I had a very loose outline. But the paragraph that preceded this one? I had no idea I would write it.

On some level, I'm not sure I even knew that I thought those things in exactly that way. I mention this because I want to acknowledge the mystery of making or creating anything before I begin to make it sound understandable. The ball often rolls with a momentum and in a direction we didn't anticipate, and that makes it seem like it comes from a source external to ourselves. In the past, we've called it inspiration, something for which we've both credited (and in its absence, blamed) the muses, the Greek goddesses responsible for the arts, literature, and science. Inspiration

CREATIVITY
IS NOT RESERVED
FOR THE EXCLUSIVE USE
OF THOSE WHO IMAGINE
THEMSELVES IN TOUCH
WITH THE MUSES.
IT'S THE RIGHT
AND PRIVILEGE
OF
EVERY
HUMAN BEING.

feel like a turnip," instead of "Today is a lovely day," then it takes practice, and at the beginning, practice is always ugly.

You should see me do yoga. I started this year, and it's the ugliest damn thing you ever saw. But it's getting better, ever so slowly.

We fear ugly, so we never start. We fear that it will never get better. We see no promise that our truly rough first attempts might become the thing we hoped for, the thing that we feel pressured to make perfect. We're scared others will see us and judge us; that our ugly first efforts will reflect back upon us. We fear we might not have the resources to pull it off, to bring it to completion. So, so many fears.

For many of us, it's the very real fear of not knowing what the next steps are. We don't have it all figured out, all we have is this spark of an idea that we can't shake, and we want to make it real, we know we can, but we don't know how. So we stall. We hesitate. We wait. For what? I'm not sure. The muses, perhaps. Inspiration?

The hardest part is beginning in the face of these fears. I try very hard not to make prescriptive statements or talk about human experiences that are universally true because there are so few of them. But as different as we all are, we have many things in common. The fundamental ways in which our brains work, for example. Basically the same, but in the details, we differ. One thing I'd be pretty close to citing as a universal principle is that everything begins in uncertainty. Even those things about which we *think* or *feel* we are certain are not. Uncertainty is unsteady ground upon which to begin something, but it's the only ground we've got.

The creative process–the way we make things–is a step-by-step process. Actually, that's an unhelpful way of looking at it because step-by-step implies each step is basically the same and it's a matter of momentum and repetition. Just put one foot in front of the other and you've got it. But that's not it at all. It's more like an improvised dance. It is iterative. One step leads to another. One move suggests the next. You can't know what the whole dance looks like until you look back on it, to see how it all came together. Each step is an uncertainty until you try it. Sometimes it works. Sometimes it doesn't. There, now I've given you a metaphor about something else I don't for a moment pretend to be able to do.

But I do know comedy. And I know improv. And what I know about that is the same as what I only *suspect* of anything in which we improvise: you never know where it's going, and what it looks like at the beginning is not remotely what it looks like when you've called it done. So while the beginning isn't *everything* in the creative process, the creative process is nothing without it. If we accept that it's almost always ugly at the beginning—if we embrace it and celebrate the rough edges and half-baked ideas and see where they lead and if we can separate those from our need to get it right, to look like we know what we're doing—then we can experience more beginnings, and stronger beginnings. Not pretty, no, but strong, necessary, speculative, take-a-deep breath-and-see-where-it-leads beginnings.

See that? 1,900 words I didn't know were coming. Sentences I had no idea I would ever write—one improvisational step in front of the other. What you don't see are all the words I deleted. That last sentence? I wrote some version of it three times before I settled on it.

Don't wait to be certain. Don't wait until you've got it all figured out before you begin. Writers don't think and then write; we write in order to think. You can't do that unless you're willing to put some words on the page, take many of them off, and move them around. And you can't do that unless you're willing to start, and for that start to be ugly. It is the same for everyone who makes anything.

Let's begin.

02
THE FEAR OF UGLY

If the secret to making things—to being creative and getting things done—is mostly in the starting, why is it so damn hard? On the surface, what could possibly be so difficult about putting paint to canvas, words on paper, or whatever it would take for you to do the things you long to have accomplished when one day you look back at your life? Why does every fresh start (or the need for one) seem to make us feel like we're about to attempt the impossible and make us look for any diversion possible in order to put it off another day?

True, some of it is just laziness. Making things takes effort. It requires that we show up and get to work in a way that staying put and staring at our phones just doesn't demand of us. It's less immediately rewarding, too. Checking social media provides the hope of that immediate dopamine hit of fresh likes, comments, connection, or affirmation—feelings that seem a long way off when we're beginning some new thing. Sure, writing a song will one day feel really good, by which I mean having *written* a song will feel good. When it's done. When the wrestling is over and we've signed our name to our creation. Few things feel like that. But there's also the possibility that this particular song doesn't go where we hoped. Like Sisyphus, our stone could just roll back down the hill and we'll have to begin again. And that scares the hell out of us. Compared to the hard soul work of making something new, taking refuge in social media is an easy out.

So, yes, it might be laziness, but I think it's more than that. I think it's fear. Primal, lizard-brain fear that whispers in our ears, "What if? What if it doesn't work out the way I hoped? What if it's a total failure? What if the thing I make isn't well-received, is misunderstood, or worse, ignored? What if the only thing I know for sure is the first step, and then it all falls apart? What if I don't have the time, the money, the talent, the energy—what if I just don't have it in me? What if I'm biting off more than I can chew with this thing? What if I'm just wasting my time with this, I mean I don't really know where it's going, do I?" And on and on.

These fears might be conscious for you, they might not, but they are there. Collectively, they've been there for thousands of years, all of them left over from a time when failing, not belonging, and not being accepted, was a life and death situation. As a race, these were very real fears at one point in our history, and the part of our brain controlling those fears had a vitally important job: keeping us alive. The moment that lizard brain (the amygdala) felt threatened, it kicked into overdrive, signaling the body to release stress hormones, quicken our breathing, narrow our vision, raise the blood pressure and push the blood to the extremities, and shut down the brain as the body gets ready to either fight or run like hell.

There are times that either fight or flight is still an important response, but standing in front of a group of 30 people and giving a 10-minute speech is not one of them.

And yet, this relatively benign activity (for God's sake, it's not 30 tigers!) counts as one of the western world's greatest fears. Why? Putting ourselves out there is scary as shit, that's why. There was a time when belonging to the tribe was everything, when conformity to the norm mattered and being ostracized (seriously, how bad do you expect that speech to be?) could mean being cast out and separated from the safety and survival that tribe represented.

We use the word "tribe" a lot these days. Almost all of us mean it metaphorically, as in, "You guys like *Star Trek* and goat yoga, too? I've found my tribe!" And when we finally do come to our senses and stop doing goat yoga or whatever phase-of-life thing we were into, it's unlikely that tribe will send us out of the camp into darkness to fend for ourselves. The crippling fear we have, even when it doesn't feel significant on a tigers-will-eat-me scale, feels very real, because it is. The amygdala is way behind in terms of evolution. Actually, it's probably right on track; it's technology and society that's far ahead of the curve, outpacing our evolution dramatically—which is probably a good thing because when evolution catches up with us, the only thing our hideously misshapen thumbs will be good for is texting.

In other words, our lizard brain is looking for dangers that no longer exist for us and haven't for a *very* long time. But it doesn't know that. Never got the memo. The fear feels real—it *is* real—even if the danger is not. Let me repeat this so you don't feel like I'm trivializing it: putting yourself out there is scary. And making things, especially making them in expectation that the world (even the small world

COURAGE
IS A CHOICE
TO LISTEN TO
THE FEAR
AND TO ACT
IN HOPES
OF PROVING IT
WRONG.

of your immediate peers or family) is always an act of putting yourself out there. In fact, it might be harder when it's "just" your friends and family because the risk is higher. There's more to lose.

There's a misconception that the size of the audience is what makes it scary, but I've found that not to be true. I spent 12 very happy years of my life performing comedy, mostly for kids and families. The largest crowd I ever performed for was at Whistler, British Columbia, on New Year's Eve as the clock ticked toward the year 2000 and we all braced for the world to end. At a conservative guess, there were 10,000 people in the audience. Ignoring for a moment that it was one of the worst performances of my life, the size of the crowd didn't make it hard. In a crowd that big, when 100 people don't think you're funny, it's a drop in the bucket. In a crowd of 30 people, if just three people don't like you, the energy can change dramatically. You can see it on their faces. It changes you as you try to pander to them, doing or saying anything to turn them into fans. But at the end of the show, no matter how bad you bomb, you're still alive. You lick your wounds, go back to your routine, and figure out how to make it stronger. The tigers are nowhere in sight.

But they feel like they are. Fear isn't logical. It's emotional. And our responses to that fear can be anything but rational. After the tragic events of 9/11 and the skies reopened to air travel, many people were too scared to get back on a plane, and instead travelled by car. The very real, very logical-feeling fear made them do it. But it wasn't logical. Statistically, the chance of being injured or killed on the highways in America is astronomically higher than being killed in a plane, much less finding yourself on one commandeered by terrorists. Car fatalities post-9/11 were noticeably higher. Sometimes the lizard brain, acting in our best interest, is the very thing that sabotages us.

So what do we do about this fear, especially in the context of a book that's about making things; a book about everyday creativity, and not about the bigger topic of fear itself? Not being a psychologist or therapist and having never walked on fire at a Tony Robbins event, all I can tell you is what has worked for me in the real world of wanting so badly to do something with my life, make some things I'm excited and curious about, and hoping the little stuff doesn't get too much in the way.

The first thing I have done is look that fear in the eye and called it by name. There was a time in my life when I was pretty angry, going through a divorce and scared I was about to lose everything. It was paralyzing. I was going to lose *everything*. And then my counsellor asked me to make a list of what *everything* was; to be specific. I filled page after page of a yellow notepad of all the things, one by one, that I feared losing. Some of it was legitimate. Yes, I might lose the couch. Hell, I might lose *both* couches. But was I losing anything that couldn't be replaced? I wasn't. Was I losing the tools by which I made a living—my creativity and comedic timing? No. Would the divorce force me to give up my jokes, my love for an audience, and my ability to market myself? My friends?

If you'll forgive me for anthropomorphizing it, fear avoids the specifics and deals in vague generalities. Standing in front of an audience giving that speech? The fear kicks in: "Don't do it! Danger! You could bomb!" But it's never very specific, is it? It never follows through. Sure, I could bomb. And then what? Someone in the audience might rightly conclude that I didn't do that very well. And then? I know once in a while the answer might be, "Then I lose my job, David; thanks for nothing!" But really? Most of the time, we sweat it out and step off the stage, glad to be done, and people tell us how great we did. We brush it off. Crisis averted. And though it might not help this one specific time, as a general response to day-to-day fear (I'm not speaking here of deep-seated phobias), it is helpful to unpack the specifics and look it in the eye rather than just stewing about it. "What's the worst that can happen?" is a very real and helpful question when you go looking for the answers rather than leaving it rhetorical. The worst is almost never that bad.

The other thing that is helpful is to become much more familiar with the things of which we are afraid. The more we fail, the more we discover our own resilience, the less we worry about the imagined consequences, and (happily) the more we enjoy the rewards.

By the end of my comedy career, I had an agent in Nashville and was doing regular shows around Canada and the U.S. Most of my audiences numbered one to two thousand people in the later years, and I loved it. *Loved* it. There is a high that comes from making that many people laugh that is genuinely hard to beat. But it was an odd career choice for the quiet kid in grade 10 who couldn't do a speech in front of his class without visibly shaking and blanking out, my autonomic nervous system in overdrive while I tried to survive the ordeal. And I did survive. And I continued to hate it. Until I started to perform for kids.

I started as a clown, something that'll get you quickly used to an audience of people that mostly hate and fear you. But I was safe behind the makeup, had access to tanks of helium, and had these beautiful little wins when a kid would smile or laugh. It was the little wins that helped. And bit by bit, I realized even the harshest audience was no threat—that they all had something to teach me. Bit by bit, I realized how harmless the roughest audience was and how easy it was to bounce back.

The same is true of diving with sharks. Yes, sharks are the apex predators of the ocean, and the first time you see one underwater, your heart quickens and you look for the exit, but as you get to understand their behaviours and you have more and more encounters with them, the fear changes. It diminishes because the uncertainty caused by ignorance or one too many shark movies as a kid gives way to knowledge and familiarity. You learn what to look for, which species are harmless, and which of them you need to behave differently with. The more you learn and experience, the more it displaces the unknown and the fear that often follows in its wake.

We are more resilient to these psychological fears than we know. I can't talk you out of them, but I can tell you the reality of them is very rarely as scary as the shadows they cast on the wall. I can tell you that most often, at least in the context discussed here, you can bounce back. And that the thing we are scared of isn't nearly as frightening as looking back on our lives—having passed so quickly our heads will spin—and wondering only then, when it's too late, what we were so scared of and why we let those fears stop us from doing the things we so badly wanted to do: things that would have opened opportunities we never got to experience and made our lives so much different. If there's one thing I am afraid of, it's allowing my fears to prevent me from living my life fully.

Perhaps there's a way to change the narrative and bring our fears on board with a new agenda, one more concerned in our daily lives with thriving than merely surviving. If we're going to listen to the fear, why not listen to fears that nudge us in the right direction? Fears based on possibilities that have a very real chance of coming true? Why do we not fear the loss of important relationships more than we fear losing face? Why not fear the loss of 40 years of our lives than the loss of a job that kills our souls? And returning to the more immediate subject, why not fear never making the art we wanted to make more than we fear the reasons we have for not putting ourselves out there and for taking a chance?

I think those are questions worth asking since the idea of living without fear at all (much as we would like it to be otherwise) isn't likely for most of us. But there is another way.

Courage. Plain old *I'm-scared-but-to-hell-with-it-I'm-doing-it-anyway* courage.

Courage isn't the absence of fear. It's not the feeling of bravery. It's turning to that part of us that is screaming, "What if this is a horrible failure?" and saying, "I have no idea, but let's find out." Stephen Pressfield, author of *The War of Art*, talks about using fear as a compass that points towards the hard, but most important, directions in our lives. I've come to see courage as three things: leaning into the fear, seeing where it leads, and one of the essential pillars of the creative life.

Courage isn't something some of us have and some do not. Courage is a choice to listen to the fear and to act in hopes of proving it wrong, and it is available to all of us, though "available" has never meant "easy." For most of us, it doesn't look like the stuff for which we win medals. For some, it's just getting out of bed or writing the first lines of the new novel. For others, it's sending the email or pressing publish on a blog post. And sometimes, it's facing the task honestly enough to know it is too big and breaking it down into pieces that are less overwhelming.

In the last few years, my mantra has been "do it anyway." It's a reminder to me that there will always be reasons not to do it (whatever *it* is). I can justify anything to myself and make it sound good, so if I want a way out of doing something, I can find it. Valid reasons abound, or they can if you give me a moment. Do it anyway. Sure, I could do it tomorrow instead of now. Do it anyway. Yes, people might hate my blog post. Hit publish anyway. Do I have any idea whether this is going to work or not? Nope. But do it anyway. And yes, it's probably going to be ugly when I start. Do it anyway.

03
THE TYRANNY OF PERFECTION

I don't like the word "perfect." Never have. It's pretentious. It's boring, and the idea that it represents things made without flaw or defect is unattainable and doesn't for a moment resonate with me. Perfect is the realm of unicorns. Maybe also dolphins. But the rest of life is a hot sticky mess, and creative efforts are even more so.

Like the fears that try to keep us safe, the goal of perfect—either in our process or the end result of our work—is a self-sabotaging goal. In fact, it's probably just another fear dressed in drag as something that's meant to sound good. Because it sounds like we should want "perfect" doesn't it? Even in high school, I was taught interview skills and told that if I was ever asked about my flaws, I should say that I could be a bit of a perfectionist. I told you it was pretentious. It's like admitting to being too noble. "Oh, me? *My* flaws? Well, I sometimes rescue too many kittens." Rubbish. Perfectionism, or the elevation and pursuit of the perfect, is the fear of the imperfect. The ugly. It's the willful, myopic, disinheriting of the flawed and the messy, the shitty first drafts, the hesitant first efforts.

Creators must not fear the messy, the bad ideas, or the disastrous first attempts at something. Not only must we not fear those things, we must run wildly towards them, arms open like a deranged lemming heading for the cliff. Lemmings, for the record, don't jump from cliffs, nor do they run headlong towards them with arms spread wide. They don't have arms. You can add this to my growing list of dodgy metaphors.

Why such enthusiasm for the ugly stuff? Two reasons. The first is that the ugly stuff is very rarely as ugly as it looks. Diamonds look pretty gross before you clean them up, too. Second, if we merely put up with ugly, we won't pursue it, and I've already told you what I think about a passive approach to creativity. We've got to chase it down. Too many people chase the perfect. And because the pre-made perfect thing doesn't exist, we'll end up sitting around waiting for it to show instead of grabbing every crappy rock we can find and polishing it until it shines or until we know there's nothing there, and we grab the next rock and start again.

The expectation of the perfect (hell, even the hope of the pretty-damn-good on the first try) stops many of us from starting at all; that's why it's dangerous. But it also stops many of us from finishing. We don't hit publish, send off the manuscript, put that piece up for sale on Etsy, or sign our name to it because it's not perfect. Creators make things. We finish them. We put them out into the world. It is not created until it's done, and as so few things in life are perfect (even after we've worked ourselves to death to make them so), we risk never being done. Seth Godin calls it shipping. You've got to ship it and move on. Start once more. But it'll never happen if you're waiting for perfect. Good, yes. Yours, certainly. Excellent, even. But perfect? That's a long wait for a train that's not coming.

Two further ideas have replaced the notion of the flaw-

CREATORS
MUST NOT FEAR THE
MESSY, THE BAD IDEAS,
OR THE DISASTROUS
FIRST ATTEMPTS AT
SOMETHING. NOT ONLY
MUST WE NOT
FEAR THOSE THINGS, WE
MUST RUN WILDLY
TOWARDS THEM.

less perfect in my mind and have helped me recalibrate my thinking and the way that I create.

The Japanese have a concept that honours imperfection, brokenness, and decay called *wabi-sabi*. There's an implicit belief that a thing gets more beautiful as it gets scarred from use and imbued with its own story. That's my own imperfect understanding of *wabi-sabi*; it too is probably rough around the edges, but I find it beautiful nonetheless, and very helpful.

What *wabi-sabi* is not is a rejection of excellence, skilled craftsmanship, and good taste. When we abandon the obsessive pursuit of perfection, we are not automatically endorsing sloppy, lazy work; perfection and excellence are not the same things. Nor are perfection and authenticity even remotely related.

Wabi-sabi is a way of embracing that; a way of saying something can be done and can be excellent not only despite the flaws—but even *because* of them. In reality, it's the nicks and scratches and the dents and mistakes—in ourselves and in what we make—that make us and our art unique. One of a kind. By definition, they are part of the personality of both the artist and the art.

There's another Japanese tradition that intrigues me. *Kintsugi* is the art of fixing broken pottery with gold lacquer, not to hide the breaks but to highlight them—to honour them. *Kintsugi* appeals to me because it feels honest. It feels like a more human approach to the unavoidable flaws, a *wabi-sabi* way of honouring the story of an object rather than discarding it, which is too often our approach to the flawed.

Wabi-sabi has been a needed shift in my perspective. The other shift came in a re-definition of the word "perfect," which can also mean "completed." Done. "Perfect," meaning without blemish, is out of my reach. But finished? Signed and shipped? I can do that, and so can you.

But how do you ship something you know isn't flawless? If *wabi-sabi* or *kintsugi* don't do it for you, try asking a different question. Forget "Is it perfect?" and try this one: "Is it me?" Does it feel right enough on this try that there's nothing more to add or take away? Does it make you happy? Did it scratch the itch for which you made it in the first place? It's easy to get hung up on questions like, "Is it good enough?" but they don't mean anything. They're a moving target at best. But, "Is it me?" That's a question I can answer. It's a question that means something to me. And because most of the time, I give myself some grace for my own rough edges, I can extend that grace to the things I make.

Because I can sign my name to it and call it done, because I've been "done" before and know I can do it again, and because I'm not afraid of the cracks but see them filled with gold, I'm more willing to start. And starting is where the magic is.

04
THE DANGER OF COMPARISON

I suspect the need for perfection is tightly tied to the way that we compare ourselves with others. We have a compulsion to know where we stand in the world, not relative to who we are, but to the tribes to which we want to belong. Just yesterday, another email came in from a sincere artist who, in so many more words, said essentially this: "I will never be a real artist, I will never be another Picasso." As though the two had anything to do with each other. As if making things—what we make, why we make, how we make it, and whether we judge it a success—has anything to do with other people. Much less a long-dead Spaniard.

And yet, human nature (and the more recent invention of social media and the pressure it brings) seems determined to make sure every moment of our lives is a moment in which we have the chance to look over our shoulders at what others are doing. There is almost no surer way of going off track.

Have you ever tried to steer a bicycle in one direction while looking somewhere else entirely for more than a moment or two? As a teenager, I got it into my head that oiling the chain on my bike would go much faster if I just did it while pedaling. Not one of my best ideas ever. When I picked myself up off the ground, I realized I had been hit by a car! A car that, on closer examination, had no driver and, once I thought about it, hadn't moved from that spot for a couple of days. Like I said, not my best idea ever.

Like riding a bike, making something requires attention to what we are doing; looking to see what others are doing and measuring our efforts against theirs guarantees two heartbreaking eventualities: never making art that is truly our own, and never becoming the person that is truly us.

The great artists in the world—no matter their field of endeavour—share this one thing: they did their thing their way. They didn't check to see what others did or how. They didn't measure what they were doing by public opinion. Tony Bourdain didn't check in to see how Jamie Oliver was cooking his brussels sprouts before he did his own. He did his thing, and if you didn't like it, too bad. Tony captured our hearts not only because of what he made as a chef or a writer, but because he did it so unapologetically his own way. That was his art. The same is true of Miles Davis, Prince, Oprah Winfrey, Freddie Mercury, David Bowie, Emily Dickinson, or Gandhi, or anyone else who has made their unique mark on the world.

Of course, it's easy to pick names from among the famous, isn't it? But remember, it's not their fame for which we celebrate them; it was their courage to be themselves. They weren't unique because they were famous—they were famous because they were unique. The fame isn't the point. In mentioning these names, I'm not suggesting we compare ourselves to them. I'm suggesting we understand that each of them was just one person, many of them born into very humble circumstances, many of them with the odds stacked against them. What put them on the path for which we now celebrate them and find meaning in what they did was a willingness to be themselves. They might finish in a blaze of glory, but they started ugly, just like we do.

A willingness to discover—and to be—yourself is the job of the artist (or the maker or creator if the word "artist" gives you a rash). The job of anyone who makes anything is to be true to the voice that called them to that task and to see creation as an exploration of that desire. It is not to make copies or imitations. And it is not to make masterpieces. That is a result, if it ever happens. It is not to make great art. Someone else will one day decide that, if it happens at all, and we have no say in it.

No, our task is to do the one thing that *is* within our control: to make things our way, and to make them unapologetically (even defiantly) ours. And then to do it again. And again. And as we do so, we get closer and closer to figuring out what it means to be us, to make work that is unmistakably us. We make the art, but it is also true that the art makes us.

In order for that to happen, we need to stop comparing ourselves to others. I suspect one of the reasons it can be so hard to start a project is because we get sidetracked, and to second-guess ourselves when we have a sense of what our first steps might be, looking to see what others are doing or how others have done or made this or that, instead of to our work.

Our eyes must always be on our work.

When we look at the work of others, what we usually see is what's *missing* in our own work. We see what we are *not*

THE GREAT ARTISTS
IN THE WORLD SHARE
THIS ONE THING:
THEY DID THEIR
THING THEIR WAY.
THEY DIDN'T MEASURE
WHAT THEY WERE
DOING BY
PUBLIC OPINION.

doing. We see awards we are *not* winning, a size of audience we do *not* have. We see that the way *they* see the world is *not* the way we see it, and we wonder what's deficient in us. And if we're trying to *be* that person, there's a lot missing. Just as they're missing some crucial pieces if they want to be us. But they don't. And it could be that the reason we look at their work and (in our better moments) celebrate it for what it is and not just use it as a point of comparison or envy is because they are looking to their work alone and not glancing over their shoulders. They are making work that is authentic.

Authenticity is a popular word right now, and like all good words, I worry that its overuse will make it meaningless. Like the word "passion," which is a formerly-favourite word of mine but has been so overused I want to roll my eyes when I hear it now, which is a shame. Everywhere we turn, someone is claiming to be passionate about something they're doing with only a little more than mild enthusiasm. Quoting *The Princess Bride's* Inigo Montoya, "You keep using that word. I do not think it means what you think it means." Passion is unmistakable. Passion means you're all in. You don't have to tell people you have it. If they don't see it in your work, you don't have it, but that's a different sermon.

To make something with authenticity means to make something that is true to who you are. It's the same idea as originality: to be true to the origins of something. Part of the sense of the word "authentic" means to do something on your own authority. The word "author" is related;

it doesn't mean someone who writes, but someone who is the *source* of the writing. Far from being merely the current word du jour, to make something with *authenticity* is the hardest thing in the world.

To make something with authenticity, to make something truly your own, is the ongoing and daily struggle. It requires that we put ourselves out there; that we bring something to the table. It requires that we show up and bare our souls. And it implies all the risks that come with that. And all the fears. And so it's no wonder that it's sometimes hard to get started on things that matter. It's also no wonder we feel something gnawing at our souls when we keep putting it off.

There is so much to be learned from other artists. I have a book beside me right now about the daily routines of writers. I read biographies of painters and writers, inventors, and musicians. It helps knowing that they struggled with the same obstacles and demons I struggle with and still managed to put something into the world that was original and authentic in the truest sense. Next to the hot mess of an individual that was Vincent van Gogh, I'm doing pretty well. It helps to know I'm not the lone delinquent in the crowd that doubts himself and his work. But learning from others is very different from comparing myself in an effort to become like them or create like them.

"The only person to whom I compare myself is myself." I've often heard those words when this conversation comes up. I used to nod my head. Yes, true, how very wise. Sagacious, even, I would think. But now I'm not so sure. I don't know anyone who's got a very clear view of themselves. The mirrors most of us look into have been so warped and cracked by years of voices pushing us this way and that. People telling us we can do anything, others telling us we can do nothing right. The years were not kind to many of us as kids, and many of us take these wounds into adulthood, believing ourselves to be the sum total of all things we were told we were—or weren't. So when you tell yourself you only compare yourself to the person you see in that funhouse mirror, I want to remind you that that is also likely an unkind and inaccurate comparison. You're looking in the wrong place.

Don't compare yourself to who you've been told you are because you probably aren't. Don't compare yourself to the person you wish you were because you probably think that person is much further away than they are. Don't compare yourself at all. Be yourself. Listen to yourself. Keep your eyes on your work. Take hold of the narrative going on in your mind, silence the voices chattering about what you *should* do and how you *should* do it, and ask yourself, "What *can* I do? How *can* I do it? What are the possibilities?" Then embrace your whim, desire, or curiosity, and follow it wherever it leads.

05
THE FAILURE OF SHOULD

When I was six years old, my parents signed me up for hockey—not something I recall having any say about, and certainly, if I know myself at all, not something I had any desire for. This would be my first and last real experience with team sports, though I didn't know that at the time. I have no real memories of this event, but then PTSD will do that to you. I also have no memories of the game being explained to me, not the purpose of the whole thing, and not the rules. But miraculously, one idea did stick: if I was unlucky enough to get the puck, I was to keep anyone else from getting it. The nuance that this "anyone else" probably only included the players on the other team and that there were acceptable, and therefore also unacceptable, ways of keeping that puck away from them, was clearly lost on me.

When the horrible day came that the puck *did* come to me, proving—at least to my young mind—that not everything happens for a reason, I panicked. Completely lost my mind. So I followed the rules; I sat on the puck. It turns out hockey does not ask you to interpret the rules so much as follow them. I learned that they're very specific about this kind of thing. I have never been good with rules. Or people yelling at me, of which there were suddenly many. "Get off the puck, kid!" This incident put a stop to any hopes my parents might have had of me going into professional sports. It also provides hints about why I am as suspicious of rules and anything dressed in the word "should."

When I teach photography, I often hear the question, "Which lens should I use?" It's sometimes replaced by, "Which settings should I use?" or, "How should I compose this picture?" That they are such common questions tells me there is a flaw in the way photography (or maybe any art) is taught, though I think it's a bigger problem than that. I think if we go all the way back to the school systems in which most of us spent our most formative years—the years in which we were laying down the most important wiring in our brains—we learned that there was a right way and a wrong way to do almost everything.

We didn't so much learn *how* to think as *what* to think. We learned how to fit in, and that we should. We learned the value of conformity but were never told what it would cost us. Many of us learned early the consequences of deviation from that path, first from teachers, and later, from bullies At the beginning of any task, we've been trained to ask, "What is expected of me?" The concern over how we *ought* to do something is so wired into many of us that it never occurs to us that the obligation ended when we left school. Or it might have had we not immediately jumped into jobs for which those schools trained us. Jobs that carried their own obligations and lists of shoulds or oughts.

I'm speaking as a bit of an outsider about employment and jobs, having graduated from theology school to become not a pastor but a comedian. After five years in two separate schools, both leaning more towards fundamentalism than I'm comfortable admitting now, I was taught more than my share of shoulds and oughts, many of them in languages I only pretended to understand. That I dropped out of Greek class to learn to juggle should tell you everything about how those years went for me. What I did learn, painfully at times, was that shoulds and oughts frown darkly on uninvited questions.

I also learned that it was the questions that were most interesting. *Shoulds* and *oughts* are about answers—most often very specific answers—and sometimes they were unwavering answers to questions we seemed to have long forgotten. My accidental journey into comedy and the fact that no church seemed to want me saved me from taking what for years my parents still called "a real job," usually in the context of, "When are you going to get one?" But friends and classmates had different paths, and I watched them go into jobs that maintained the obligation to follow the *shoulds* and the *oughts*.

It's not my intention to judge the choices others make about their jobs. Not everyone should be a comedian; there were people in my audiences who were pretty sure I was among them. But it's worth understanding the pattern. There's value in looking back at our lives and seeing the slow but persistent chipping away of the thoughts and behaviours that made us stand out and to see the slow erosion of the finer edges of our individuality and creative thought. It's easy to see the way our questions turned to answers and, once in possession of those answers, the loss of the ability to press on with further questions.

Questions of *should* and *ought* free us from the uncer-

IF
THE FIRST
QUESTION WE
ASK OURSELVES
IS, "HOW SHOULD
I START THIS THING?"
I THINK WE'RE
ALREADY
DOOMED.

tainty of more creative and individual thought. They have their place in building a society, constructing buildings and laws; please don't mistake me, I'm not asking you to start burning tires in the streets. I think creative individuals make stronger global citizens, not sociopaths. I'm not suggesting you abandon your social conscience and start driving on the wrong side of the road.

I'm suggesting we're addicted to getting answers because it's easy and we've been trained to do so. And the problem with answers is we stop asking questions once we find them. "What should I do?" when applied to the novel you are writing or the dance you are choreographing will find an answer. It will. You're a creative person; you'll solve the problem. But it could also be that the first answer to that question, though it seems the right one, isn't as strong as it might have become if you had kept asking better questions. "What should I do?" isn't remotely as powerful a question in uncovering possibilities as "What *can* I do?"

That. Right there. That's the point. What do we *get* to do? *What are the possibilities?* How can we approach this differently? What if my assumptions are all wrong? What if it's not this or that but some combination of this *and* that? All of these questions serve us more faithfully than the previous questions. All of them lead us to new possibilities, and all of them require us to test them out, to fail a couple of times, and in doing so, to find even more questions and more possibilities.

To do this requires a certain amount of defiance or a willingness to resist the tractor beam of conformity and homogeny. It requires a willingness to stand out rather than blending in. Yes, that takes courage, but this isn't about being different for the sake of being different; it's mostly about being faithful to who you are and asking your own questions rather than settling for the answers of others.

Isn't this a book about getting started and being more creative in the truest sense of the word? Making more, getting more done, and shipped? It is. And if the first question we ask ourselves is, "How *should* I start this thing?" I think we're already doomed. The alternative is simple and powerful: replace obligation or any sense that there's a right or wrong way to do this, with possibility and questions that reflect that. Replace it all—even for those of you doing client work (I'll discuss constraints later)—with better questions: What do you *want* to make? What would be interesting for you, exciting for you? Where is your curiosity leading you? What crazy, bold, idea would you entertain if no one was looking over your shoulder? How would *you* like to do this? What excites you?

Then look for possibilities and not answers. When we find an answer, we stop asking the question. Done. The exploration stops. But possibilities require us to play with them and see where they lead. Possibilities get us from the undeveloped ideas and the low-hanging fruit, to the stronger ideas and more interesting questions. Answers stop the flow. Never stop the flow.

06
THERE IS NO MAP

Flow is a state in which the ideas come free and easy, or so it seems. It's the high of the writer for whom the chapter just emerges onto the page. It's the lost time of the songwriter who, hours after she has sat down to work, looks up from a song that until now never existed, and feels like no time at all has passed. It's that time in the studio when every stroke of the brush feels right. And it's the reason we long believed in the power of the muses and the idea of inspiration because it all feels so magical.

But we have to get there first; we have to strike out into the unknown territory on which every act of making a thing begins. That unknown territory is different for us all. For some, it's the blank page, for others the silence not yet filled with song, or a stage and a waiting audience. But for all of us, that emptiness is calling: Start. And if you're like me, you'll respond with "Where?"

It is human nature to want a map. We want to look down and see it all laid out before us. That red dot is where I am now. The other is where I want to end up. And here, the most direct path between them marked with a yellow highlighter so I don't get confused. It's all so easy.

But the problem with maps is that they depend on knowing the territory and, if you plan to use one to navigate, then you need to know the destination. When we make anything, we never know the destination, and we rarely know the territory. But we think we know. Many of us have an idea in our heads, something we've visualized and thought about so often it feels almost real. And it is those expectations that can trip us up.

As a photographer, I've learned that what we expect to see blinds us to what is actually there. When I was still an entertainer and studied sleight of hand, the first lessons I learned taught me how much goes on where the audience isn't looking. In fact, so much more goes on in the spaces where we aren't looking and aren't expecting anything to happen than where we do. We miss so much when we're focused on what we expect and looking for the map.

If there were a map to our creative process, it would rob us of one of the great joys of creating and would stop us from getting to the unexpected places that so many of us, once done, credit for the work becoming what it is: serendipity and the discovery of new directions and possibilities.

There is no map, but what we have is so much better. We know how to get to flow. And if we know how to get to flow, then starting gets much easier; it's free from the paralyzing need to know exactly where we're going but comes with the freedom to focus instead on *how* we are going.

Flow requires four things: time, attention, skill, and challenge. When you put your head down to do something, free from distraction, and that something challenges the level of the skill with which you make it, flow occurs. Rather, it *can* occur. We all need different amounts of time: time to ramp up our creative thinking and shake the dust off; time to gain momentum. We all ebb and flow with the levels of attention we can give and the distractions we allow. And the mix of skill and challenge is always changing, so this isn't so much a recipe we follow as it is a dance we participate in.

Follow me a little further on this detour; we'll get back to the map (and its conspicuous nonexistence) in a moment. We'll explore time and attention later, but for now, consider the role that challenge plays in attaining flow. Creativity, however else you want to define it, is ultimately just problem solving. It's the brain's process of combining ideas in the real world, and in order for it to work, it needs a problem to solve—something to chew on. That's the engine of our creative efforts; without something interesting to chew on, it loses interest. The muse gets bored, petulant, and lazy.

Challenge happens when the level of our skill is just a little outpaced by our vision for the thing we're making—when we fight just a little out of our class. That's when the sparks fly. Take on something that's not interesting enough, that's not a challenge, or that doesn't make you question whether you can pull this off, and you'll get bored and rely on past efforts and well-worn paths. You will not do your best work there. And if you take on something too big, you'll get frustrated because your resources just truly aren't equal to the task, and you won't do your best work there, either.

If we want to get to flow with any consistency, our vision must always outpace our craft. But our craft must always be growing, keeping up, if only always a step behind. It's in that space where we flow and do our best work.

KNOWING
HOW TO GET
TO FLOW
IS MUCH MORE
IMPORTANT
THAN KNOWING
WHERE YOU'RE
GOING.

Back to the map metaphor. The only maps that exist in the creative world are templates. Formulae and recipes. Paint-by-numbers is a map. You didn't start reading this book because you don't know how to paint by numbers. You started this book, at least in part, because you hunger for more. The thing you hunger for, I suspect, is a greater familiarity with flow and a better understanding of how to get there. I think if more of us knew how to get to flow as part of our everyday working-class kind of creativity, starting would be easier because we would know that flow isn't magic, and it doesn't need a map.

You do not need to know where you're going; that will be revealed to you as flow happens. If you can trust me on that, stick that promise in your back pocket while you finish the book and I'll make it worth your while. For now, consider a change in your thinking and a shift in focus from, "How do I get there?" (because not being able to answer that will prevent you from starting) to, "Let's see where this leads!"

Every act of creation is wildly speculative: it's a great big series of what-ifs and a willingness to explore around the blind corners to which a state of flow most reliably leads. We would all be so much more at ease in the making and in the starting (and enjoy it all so much more!) if we let go of our expectations and were more open to seeing where it all leads. That doesn't mean we let go of our hopes, our longings, or the ideas that got us to the point of starting. It means we hold them with an open hand and lean into the excitement of discovery, checking the specific expectations at the door.

Too often, our focus is on getting it done, on signing the work—and shipping it. Shipping matters, but not at the beginning. At the beginning, a focus on the end product needs to take a back seat to the process of making that thing and needs to come with full permission to take the scenic route and the detours, to put the top down and enjoy the unexpected. I don't want to get too zen on you, but we've got to be a lot more in the here and now when we create. To enjoy this moment, this challenge, without laying our expectations on top of them. There is a time to flow and a time to course-correct, and those times are mutually exclusive.

When we are making, every day is a new beginning. When I sat down to write this morning, it was not so much a continuation of an existing process; you can't just jump back into flow. This chapter was a new start. And what I began with was not a map for getting to *done* on this chapter, nor a sense of exactly what it needed to look like. I started with just a sense of what this chapter needed to do and the pit-of-my-stomach feeling of, "Well, I wonder where the hell this is going to go?"—a feeling that can be experienced as either negative or positive, depending on what you look for. I choose to look at it as an adventure. I know that if I sit down and begin writing, that my first words, ideas, and whole paragraphs will be ugly. They must be. Their job is to be ugly and grease the wheels. But they'll lead me somewhere.

They always lead me somewhere. Not because I have a map, but because I have something more important. I have put time aside, I am careful with my attention, and I've learned that the flying-by-the-seat-of-my-pants feeling isn't something to scare me off but an indication that I'm at the intersection of my craft as a writer and my vision for the direction of this book.

I've also accepted that right now, as I write, my job is not to edit, not to clean up the mistakes and the mess; if anything, it's to make more of them and see where they lead. There will be time to edit, to rewrite whole paragraphs, even whole chapters. But I will never get there if I keep looking down at a map of my own making, taking myself out of the only one way of creating and doing my work that has ever worked: *flow*. Knowing how to get to flow is much more important than knowing where you're going, because you never really do. But flow will show you.

07
RESPONSE:ABILITY

Creativity—the process of making things—is not linear, but it is iterative. One idea leads to another, and that idea suggests something else. At each junction (you say failure, I say junction), we respond and make choices. They are not always easy choices (though there's usually less riding on them than we think), but they are our choices alone to make. This is what it means to be responsible. The word "responsibility" didn't start out implying accountability, but rather the capacity to respond. To pivot, change directions, to add to, or remove from, the current effort, to not judge it based on what it is now (it's not finished!) but to entertain thoughts of what might be. Each chance to respond, to make a choice, is a chance to refine.

Despite the magical feeling of it, flow is not a state of being or working that comes from external sources. In the literal sense, the muse has nothing to do with it. In the metaphorical sense, she only shows up when you do; she has to find you working. Everything in the creative life, all of it, depends on us. The muse is handy if we need a scapegoat, but if "the inspiration doesn't show up," it's no one's fault but our own. Writer's block doesn't exist. Not in the way that is implied, as though it's an external thing that just bumped into us, a force to which we are unwitting victims. As if by claiming "writer's block" (or whatever version you get as a potter or a sculptor or a composer), you're saying you hit a patch of bad weather over which you have no control; weather that you have no choice but to wait out and hope it passes. Just a passive victim. Nonsense.

At some point, the creative life brings you to the realization that you have agency—that anything you make or do is entirely up to you. For many of us, it's what we love so much about being creative and making things. Yes, it's the scratching of an itch that we can't relieve any other way and it's the joy of seeing something made, and not only made, but made by *our* hands. The result of *our* mind at work. A thing that is somehow greater than the sum of our choices, but which wouldn't have been realized in this way without each of those decisions. *Our* decisions.

Art (or again, Life, if you don't see your work as art) is about choices—the choice to sit down and get to work: hands on the clay, the paintbrush, the keyboard. The choice to follow your whim down any random alley, to back out when it goes nowhere or take a left when it forks. The choice to tell one story rather than another, and to tell uncomfortable truths in that story, if that's where it takes you. On the most basic level, it's choices as simple as whether to use red instead of blue just because you want to. Every moment of the day, in the making of whatever it is you make, is about choice.

Some people recognize this before they begin, and it paralyzes them. Frozen in fear, they do nothing. We've all been at the junction wondering which way to go, worried that a wrong choice will lead to more and more wrong choices that take us further from the thing we're meant

WHEN
WE ARE
AT THE
BEGINNING,
THE ONLY
TRULY WRONG
CHOICE
IS
NOT
STARTING.

to be making, the artist we are meant to become. We see each decision as if it's life-alteringly important. It's not; life isn't like that. When we are at the beginning, the only truly wrong choice is *not* starting.

When did we start taking this stuff so damn seriously? As kids, we drew purple horses. We drew hundreds of drawings just to make them and move on. We chose colours based on whim or some internal logic only accessible to children, but from which we could all benefit as adults, if only we could still access it. Kids know they have choices but aren't paralyzed by them. Kids haven't yet learned to make every decision so binary: I choose *this* to the exclusion of choosing *that*. One is right, one is wrong. Are you kidding? They choose this *and* that all the time. Draw a purple horse! Then draw an orange one! And then draw one with two heads!

We didn't stop drawing orange two-headed horses because we came to the realization that they don't exist. We stopped because someone told us they don't exist in a way that implied we should draw only what we see. We should do it *right*. To do otherwise is *wrong*. We should colour within the lines. So we began to make choices based on a learned fear of ridicule. We began to conform. We chose to listen to the voice of authority rather than the voice of our imagination. We abdicated, and many of us haven't stopped doing so. Those of us that *have* stopped abdicating still find it a daily struggle, the contrary voices still ringing in our ears.

How you make your art—even whether you make it at

all—is no one's choice but your own, no matter what the voices tell you. It is *your* choice to begin that work and let it be really ugly for a while. It is also your choice to keep doing so when it's not easy. Writer's block is code for "I got stuck. It got hard. And I stopped making choices."

You always have choices. To try something else, scrap the whole damn thing and start again, to do more research, to try a new project for a while, to problem solve and work that thing like a rented mule. And yes, to give up and stare at the page. I don't mean to browbeat the downtrodden here (God knows I've been there), but to encourage you; if it's a choice to remain stuck, it's also a choice to start over— to get unstuck. The muse isn't coming until you show up.

Here's why this matters: if you look at the particular creative project you're about to start, the one you're dragging your feet on, and you see it as a series of linear choices that all depend on that first big step forward, then that first step is going to feel scary as hell. Especially if you think (even unconsciously) that the creative path is a one-way street. But it's not. You must not be afraid of starting ugly, but you also must not be afraid of starting over. And over. And over. Your job is not to make the finished thing; the process will take care of that. It'll happen. Your job is to explore, to risk, to try, until you hit the sweet spot when you see the hints of a diamond under the rougher materials—until you feel that spark ignite in your gut.

The creative process is almost never linear, though it often looks (misleadingly) that way in hindsight. In fact, because we think we see so clearly in hindsight, it's easy to

THAT
FINAL
WONDROUS
THING YOU
MAKE DEPENDS
NOT SO MUCH
ON HOW YOU
BEGIN BUT
THAT
YOU BEGIN
IT.

look back at past projects and falsely remember them to have been so much easier than the one we're working on now. We forget the fog, the time we spent bumping around in the dark and the missteps all to get to a finished thing that we couldn't really see. But looking back, we see it all so clearly: the thing that we made, the way each choice was so obviously necessary. It looks like a road map now that we've made the journey. "Of course," we say. "Of course it ended up like this. How could it have been otherwise?" But it could. It always can. And you can't expect the clarity you felt at the end of the last thing you made to be present at the beginning of the current thing.

That expectation screws us up. Because we lack the clarity, because we don't see the path, we fear making those first choices and beginning.

Here's what I know: *that* you make a choice is more important than which specific choice you make because it's very rare that any of the single things we do carries the kind of consequences we think they do. It's rare that starting ugly doesn't show us some new thing, bring us new ideas, and give us the direction we wanted before we started. That's how it works. You start tentatively, speculatively, knowing the first steps are going to be wobbly, that you might bang into some walls, even fall down, but that those steps contain the lessons you need to refine, and to redirect. Understanding this isn't enough; you have to embrace it, go all in.

Do not abdicate your creative life to others, to the hope of incoming inspiration, or to whomever your muse is. Take responsibility. Know that starting is not the only choice, that it doesn't cast the dye and commit you to one path or another, that you can change your mind—respond!—at any time. That final wondrous thing you make depends not so much on *how* you begin but *that* you begin it.

08
WRITE DRUNK, EDIT SOBER

The moment we begin anything, we start hearing voices. One of those voices is your own, the voice that pushed you to begin, to make whatever it is you've just this moment begun. One of those voices might also be fear. Another might be your father telling you it's not good enough or that *you* aren't good enough. Still another might be the imagined voices of all the people you admire, accumulated and overbearing, telling you it's cliché, it's derivative, it's too obvious, it's too cryptic. And on and on.

Those voices are all part of you. Like fear, they are worth listening to for what they offer that is helpful. Our fears, listened to at the right time (though not necessarily obeyed), can push us in the direction we most need to go. The voices that tell us it's not good enough, when listened to at the right time (though not obeyed), can nudge us toward excellence. The voice of the jerk that left an Amazon review that said "the author seems overly fond of words" can be used to keep us conscious of the value of a tighter edit. These voices can be a balancing force in our work when used well and intentionally.

Listening is not obeying. It's considering. It's taking the useful and leaving the toxic. When my first books were published, I was very defensive. I was also foolish enough to read my reviews on Amazon and take them personally. I took it all to heart, both the good and the bad. Some reviews put me on a mountaintop. Others crashed me back to Earth. What I did not do was sift through the reviews to find what was useful in them to become better at what I do. Much of the praise was as bad for me as the sharp criticism. I could have done more filtering. I could have asked more often, "Is there something here I can use?"

That does not mean that the guy who tells me I'm long-winded gets to tell me how to do what I do. It means I acknowledge that I'm no Hemingway. Hemingway was brief. To the point. He wrote sentences that were simple. Like this. He didn't go for a lot of adjectives and adverbs. I am not Hemingway, and there's a good chance I will never please that critic no matter how tightly I edit my work; he is clearly not my audience. Do I feel any pressure at all to be more like Hemingway? Not on your life. But could there be value in tightening things up? Would that help me make stronger work that is also a tighter version of me? Perhaps. Take the useful, leave the rest.

Since we've invited him into the conversation, it was Hemingway himself who gave the timeless advice to "write drunk, edit sober." Having read a couple biographies of the man, it wouldn't be much of a stretch to think he was being literal. The man liked his drink. He was also extremely disciplined, rising at 5:30 or 6:00 a.m. every morning to write, standing up, and tracking how many words he had written. This kind of routine and work ethic is not the behaviour of a man who just stumbled in and wrote his words in a drunken blur before collapsing into his bed or, more likely, another martini. When asked about whether he mixed his drinking with his writing, he famously replied, "Jeezus Christ! Have you ever heard of anyone who drank while he worked? You're thinking of Faulkner. He does sometimes—and I can tell right in the middle of a page when he's had his first one."

So when Hemingway urges us to write drunk and edit sober, he's telling us there's a time for creating and a time for critiquing. There is a time to listen to your voice, and only your voice, to be drunk in the way Charles Baudelaire begs us in his poem, Be Drunk: "It is time to be drunk! So as not to be the martyred slaves of time, be drunk, be continually drunk! On wine, on poetry or on virtue as you wish!" He is pleading with us to be alive, to feel the wonder of it, to let it take us away, stumbling. To be a little too loud, use too many damn words (if that's what we like), and colour outside the lines. He is begging us not to be restrained, and to listen to our own voice. He is begging us to start a little ugly, telling us there will be time to make it pretty, to tighten things up and (forgive me for putting it this way, but the metaphor demands it) to clean the vomit off the floor now and then.

It's only a metaphor. But do you see the freedom in those words? To create with the kind of abandon or curiosity or speculation, to write long paragraphs that just feel right at the time, all the while telling those other voices (while possibly slurring a little) to "Just shut the hell up; I'm working here!" Those other voices will have their time. You'll hear them out. Some will contain something useful; some will be heard and dismissed. And yes, once in a while, you'll tell

OUR
FEARS
CAN PUSH
US IN
THE DIRECTION
WE
MOST
NEED
TO
GO.

them to fuck off.

There is a time to do the messy work, the work of beginning, of getting the paint on the canvas and the angst into the song. A time of false starts and fumbled first steps. There's a time to throw caution to the wind. That time must not be mixed with the time to hone the work and bring a more critical eye to it. There's a time to listen to the voice that comes from the deepest-down places in you and a time to listen to the sharper voices; those times are not the same.

We will make better, stronger, more authentic work when we do not judge the work as we make it. This doesn't mean we do it without thinking. It's not mindless work I'm advocating, but intentional work that's driven by whatever urge inside you that pushes you to make—with full permission to split the act of making into a wildly messy exploratory stage and a stage concerned with polishing. When we don't do it this way, the voices that are concerned with polishing get really loud when the mess is being made and they inhibit us, stopping us from starting at all.

That does not mean we do A and then B, and we're done. I don't mean to imply that it's this simple. Most of us will bounce back and forth more than once as we make something. We write drunk, edit sober, and then grab the metaphorical bottle and rewrite, then sober up again to edit, back and forth over the life of the work until the drunk writer and the sober editor agree that they've done their best and it's time to sign it and move on. It's a messy process with some tidying up in the middle. But the writer and the editor—the creator's voice and the critical voice—must each stick to their assigned tasks. This applies to writing, but also to every creative effort. Make while drunk and carried along by flow; refine while sober.

Suppressing the voices has never worked for me, in part because they are a part of me, for better or for worse. But giving them each a chance to be useful, at the most useful time in the process, has helped tremendously. It stops (or quiets) the noise that can happen when they're all clamouring at once. But make no mistake, without therapy, those voices won't be silenced in the day-to-day making of the things that matter to us; they will insist on being heard. So listen to them at the right time, take what's helpful, and leave the others to mumble to themselves while you get back to work. And when they're all yelling at you because your first efforts are ugly, remind them they're meant to be ugly; that's how it works. They'll have their time to weigh in. And most importantly, you'll have your start.

09
CREATORS, NOT CREATIVES

Creativity is a funny word. It's fuzzy around the edges—one of those words no one seems to be really clear on. Other words are easy. You say the words "bridge." "cat," or "turnip," and people know exactly what you mean. Say the word "creativity" or "creative," and it's really hard to pin it down, like trying to nail Jell-O™ to the wall. Even harder is the word "creative" when used as a noun rather than an adjective, as in, "Oh, Kevin doesn't have a *real job*—he's a *creative*." *Creative* is an adjective; it describes the thing we do or the way we do things, but not *what* we do. It's a lousy noun.

I know this is just splitting hairs, but the thing is, how we use our words is how we think. When I talk to people about being creative, the first response is, "Oh, I'm not that creative," as if what I meant was that kind of wild originality people associate with abstract art, or avant-garde dance, or a tendency to wear purple leggings. It's the same response I get when I talk about art as well, but in that case, I think people just want to distance themselves from the overly-precious use of the word, as if to claim our work as *art* is something only the most pretentious among us would do. So the words can be problematic, and if the words aren't clear, neither is the thinking.

It is amazing the clarity that can come in our choice of words. When I talk about "the creative process," does it sound a little mystical, a little unattainable? What if we re-framed it and instead talked about the way we make things and the way we *think* about making things? Doesn't that sound more approachable, like you could wrap your brain around it and we could all know what it meant? Doesn't it sound a little more blue-collar, less lofty, and more attainable? When it's less of a mystery, it's a little easier to wade in.

Somewhere along the line, creativity got separated from its roots as a thing we do: a dirt-under-the-nails, get-to-work-and-get-your-head-out-of-the-clouds kind of activity. When creativity stops being a work ethic, it gets a lot harder. Harder to understand. Harder to talk about. Harder to do. Combine that with all this talk about inspiration (not something we do) and muses (not something we control), and it's no wonder we often feel like this is all just completely out of our hands when the opposite is true.

Creating (and making) is a work ethic: a way of working and bringing new things into the world. It has as much to do with the hands as with the brain. Creative thinking is merely problem-solving. To put it crassly—and in terms most *creatives* would likely cringe at—we are producers. We produce. Yes, at our best, the things we produce come from the deeper parts of us and reflect something of our humanity, of wonder and beauty, among a great many other things. They contain a part of us. But at the end of the workday, it is a thing to be made, and if humans are good at anything (often to our detriment), we are very good at finding ways to make things when we get to work.

IDEAS
ARE STILL
NOTHING
BUT SPARKS
IN THE BRAIN
UNTIL WE
FLESH THEM OUT
AND GET THEM
INTO
THE
REAL
WORLD.

Everyday creativity doesn't happen by accident. It is not just a matter of "coming up with good ideas." Creating, or *being* creative, is not merely ideation. It is not just how we *think*, though that has been the focus of this book to this point. Important as they are, as the source of everything we do, ideas are still nothing but sparks in the brain until we flesh them out and get them into the real world. The real world is where they take shape and find both their initial speculative forms—the sketches, the rough drafts, the prototypes—as well as the thing they finally become as they are combined, refined, and evolve.

Any discussion of creativity that focuses on ideation and not on the real-world realities of time, attention, constraints, and the *how* of making things would be incomplete and would only encourage the armchair creatives whose bold motto always seems to be, "I could have done that!"

Ideas are raw materials, but nothing more. As we'll see, single ideas aren't even the raw materials so much as they are *component* materials. It's rare that "I have an idea!" gets translated into a final thing without first being combined with other ideas, many of them ideas that, at first glance, we might disregard as "bad ideas." But the idea that's not useful on its own often leads to better ideas or combinations of ideas that *are* useful. In my experience, that mash-up happens most often (and most usefully) in the real world. This is the fuzzy threshold, the liminal space between ideation and creation, and the steps we take here are some of the most exciting.

The next half of this book concerns the pragmatic—

moving beyond how we think to what we do. Neither is more important than the other, though how and what we think is usually the way things start. Left in the realm of thought, however, is where too many of our projects remain for too long. It is only action that gains momentum for us, that uncovers new ideas, turns bad ideas into better, helps us focus on real problems rather than imaginary, and converts "what if?" into actual tactics and tools for starting—whether that's beginning the ideation or planning process with a pencil and a notebook, the first tentative moves, the messy bits in the middle, or the final push to completion. There is no creativity without doing.

10
THE VALUE OF BAD IDEAS

For creative people, everything begins with an idea. A spark. A "what if?" moment that sets miracles in motion and begs us only to see it through. Or that's the notion. I've found this to happen about as often as the tooth fairy visits. It is extremely rare that an idea just comes out of nowhere, the animated lightbulb illuminating above our heads, which is a damn shame if you ask me because we'd all have much less trouble getting things done and starting on projects if we could trust the power of epiphany.

The trouble is that, like most things we create, whether that's art or a product or a marketing campaign (the latter two might also be art, depending on how precious you are about the definition), ideas come to us iteratively, in an evolutionary mash-up of some often very bad or half-baked notions. Much like humans themselves do, our ideas often start ugly. In my own creative process, I often hear the words or think to myself, "I have a bad idea, but I'm going to say it anyway," and I hear that much more often than, "I've got a great idea!" In point of fact, it is often those so-called great ideas that turn out to be some of the most anaemic, and the real skill comes not in having ideas, but in recognizing the potential in each of them and separating the so-called good from the so-called bad.

But how do you do that? Without wanting to seem like I'm backtracking, I wonder if it begins by not seeing ideas as good or bad at all, but rather as potential and possibility. When we too-quickly judge our ideas as positive or negative, we encounter two dangers. The first is that we discard the bad ideas before they have a chance to lead somewhere interesting. When we throw out the ideas that are uglier than others and appear to have less potential, we discard raw materials that might have been combined with others and made into something unexpected and truly good a little further down the line. The other danger is that seeing an idea you judge to be good and clinging onto it and refusing to second-guess your assessment of that idea as good, you can blind yourself to further iterations, combinations, and possibilities. In other words, most ideas start ugly, and you can neither neglect them for being so nor turn a blind eye to their ugliness and not ask more from them, without losing something.

Thinking creatively is an exercise in improvisation, and improvisation done well depends on neither giving up too soon on the bad ideas nor on camping out too quickly on the good. There are very few ideas that are so bad they can't lead to something more interesting or combined with something else to make them viable. And there are very few ideas that seem so really and truly great you can't believe you thunk them that can't be improved.

For me, this is the fun part of what I do. When I can let go of my tendency to be so binary about the ideas I have, it leads to exploration. I do that with questions. For the bad ideas, I ask myself questions like:

- What piece of this made me think this was a good idea?
- What makes this idea so bad or non-viable?
- What could I take away from this or add to it that might make it more viable?
- Is it just the timing that's wrong?

And because the last chapter ended with the affirmation that creativity was about doing, I put those questions and their replies into my notebook. I write them down. The same is true of the good ideas, and I treat my judgment with no less suspicion by asking:

- What makes me so sure this idea is good or viable?
- Would it be improved by taking something away or adding something?
- Is now the right time for this idea?
- What immediate opportunities or obstacles might this idea face?

Those are not the only questions. Your immediate context might suggest many more. The point is that we submit them to scrutiny and rigor and never as though they emerged from our minds whole and complete. They are raw materials only and it would be a shame to waste them by being too presumptuous with them. And you must never let them go.

The person you are in this moment will look at the ideas

you're having now from a very particular angle. Maybe you haven't had enough coffee. Perhaps you've had too much. Maybe you're worried about something that's forcing you to see things through a certain emotional filter. It could be there are needs in your life right now—problems that you are trying to solve—that this idea or the other don't perfectly solve. This doesn't make the idea or the approach to your current project a bad one; it might just make it a poor fit. But in six days or six months, you'll be looking to solve a different problem for which that idea might be perfect. Or you might have learned something critical in the time in between that allows you to see it from a new angle. Or in those converging days or months, you might have come up with several other incomplete ideas that now make perfect sense together.

If you throw out the bad ideas and do not give them a place to accumulate and age, you'll have discarded some of the most treasured resources of the creative process. Your ideas will often start ugly, and you can't toss them out because you're too short-sighted to see that they, or you, might change.

This is where an Ugly Notebook comes in. If this book in your hands is to be of any value, I think it needs to be pragmatic as much as it aims to be poetic. I want it to be about what you do and not only what you think, so I'm urging you to get an Ugly Notebook.

I have many notebooks. Beside me now on a shelf are 40 little black Moleskine™ notebooks, though the brand doesn't matter. They're pocket-sized with lined paper, held closed

IF YOU THROW
OUT THE
BAD IDEAS
AND DO NOT
GIVE THEM A PLACE
TO ACCUMULATE
AND AGE,
YOU'LL HAVE DISCARDED
SOME OF THE MOST
TREASURED RESOURCES
OF THE
CREATIVE PROCESS.

with black elastic that's now stretched and lost its bounce. And in them, I write my thoughts and my ideas. Part journal, part mental sketchbook, you'll rarely see me without one. But a couple of years ago, I noticed something about my approach to these notebooks: I was being precious with them. I hesitated to write an idea unless it was reasonably well-articulated and more than halfway formed. Anything that might get scratched out, any diagram that might need to be re-drawn, a brainstorm I wasn't sure would go anywhere, or a list I thought I might not complete, I didn't risk putting it in my notebook. And that's a problem.

It's a problem because creatively, I depend on the ugly, the half-baked, and the what-was-I-thinking? So while others might have reacted to this by simply taking their notebooks less seriously and treating them less preciously, I knew that was a battle I'd lose. Fighting tendencies that are long and deep for us is rarely productive and takes us out of flow rather than letting it continue. I don't want to spend my energy causing chaos in my process, so I bought an Ugly Notebook. That's what I call it. It's the same as my others (though larger) so it can accommodate drawings and scribbles and brainstorms. Unlike the others, the whole point of it is to let it be ugly.

My Ugly Notebook is where all my worst ideas and the ones that currently aren't going anywhere sit and wait for me to gain some perspective, for the times to change, or for me to ask better questions of them. It's a place where anything goes. I can say anything, think anything, and ask any question. I make lists. Endless lists. Ten ideas for my next book. Ten ways to make $1,000. Possible topics for my podcast. And I cross things out and ask questions. Would this book be better as a video series or a course? Is this just one book or two? Am I thinking too big? Too small? Endless questions.

But that's where I start. Almost any project now begins at some point with a scribble or the unexpected answer to an idea I thought was stale, but was sitting there waiting for me in my Ugly Notebook. And I re-read the notes often. I write them down because that helps me think. It's amazing what starts coming out when I sit down and scribble. So for its own sake, the Ugly Notebook serves an immediate purpose—but it is also an archive. A repository. A nursery for all my ugly babies. For that to have value, you need to go back to them, revisit them, and wonder at their growth. Poke them to see if they're still alive. I've very often closed that book with an idea in hand that I'd once rejected and moved forward on it to make of it something interesting, even good. This book also began there.

The idea that there are no bad ideas, and that all ideas need a place to get beyond their often ugly first appearances, is not only for the lone artist or the person who identifies as creative. It's for everyone—teams, too. In my business life (which I try very hard not to separate from my creative life because business is a very creative pursuit for me), I find myself talking to my wife or my manager, and one of us will often say, "OK, this is a bad idea, but I'm going to say it anyway." Because we know that even the best ideas won't come out fully formed and the ones that seem like the runts of the litter might grow new legs and evolve into something different when someone else adds their two-cents worth by saying, "That's interesting; what if we…?"

Perhaps the most helpful thing we can all do is stop talking about ideas in binary terms at all. Instead of "good" or "bad" ideas, what if we thought and spoke of ideas on a spectrum from incomplete to refined, or from young to mature? From raw material to finished concept? What if the worst of our ideas were valued, kept somewhere safe, and revisited often enough that they had a chance to become more than they first appeared to be? I think if we saw our ideas this way, we might find it easier to start, and not only easier but more productive, more open to possibility and the kind of improvisation that has always been part of turning initial ideas into more refined ideas and eventually better outcomes, whatever it is we're making.

However, ideas only become fully realized—only become an actual thing—when they are hammered out in the real world where they have a chance to encounter reality and continue their evolution away from ugly and toward whatever thing it is you're bringing into the world. To do that takes action: small, manageable steps that lead to little wins, proof of concept, and momentum.

11
SMALL STEPS / LITTLE WINS

This book began in my Ugly Notebook but didn't stay there long before moving to my To-Do List in Evernote (one of the few apps I don't think I could live without), which is where actionable items that come out of my Ugly Notebook end up. On that list was "Write New Book (Start Ugly?)" next to a little empty checkbox, as though I might have woken up on Wednesday, gone to get milk (check), answered some emails (check) and then written my book (check) before moving on to something else, perhaps emptying the trash.

No one I know works like that. If that one actionable item had forever remained on the To-Do List in that form, it never would have happened. It's too big. It's overwhelming. And there is no clear next step by which to begin the project. And big, overwhelming, and vague are the reasons procrastination is so common and easy for us. When I look down the barrel of things I need to do, I almost always choose those that are either most urgent or those that are small and easy. I tackle the thing I can get my head around before that big, uncertain project with really fuzzy edges, and I'm betting you do, too.

My mother recently called me a workaholic. She was kidding (oh, God–I *hope* she was kidding). Others tell me I'm prolific, which I think is their way of saying the same thing as my mom, only nicer. Being seen like that, I think it's probably easier to explain away how I get so much done, as though it's just part of my genetic code, some weird aberration in my DNA that makes sense of my productivity. But you should know that left to my own devices, I am lazier than a cat in a sunbeam. I have a couch in my office just so I can take long naps and, for as long as I can and as much as possible, avoid hard work. So don't go pinning any of that superhero crap on me. In fact, I think it's my proclivity to lean away from big, seemingly unmanageable projects (while also needing to put food on the table and wanting to keep my wife in the style to which she is accustomed) that makes it so much easier for me to get things done when they are divided up into the smallest pieces possible.

When I sit down to write a book or create a new product or do any project that's more daunting than flossing my teeth or putting a glass in the dishwasher, and I see that the next step is something I can get done in three hours or less, it's an easy win; I get to put a tick in the checkbox, and those little ticks are like a hit of heroin (or they might be—I've never done drugs). But dopamine, perhaps? And it feels great. It feels like progress and forward momentum, and it makes me want more. I know this about myself.

When we take small steps—steps that are well-defined and manageably acted upon—those small steps either give us the confidence to keep moving or show us early hints that the thing we're working on is neither overwhelming nor a complete disaster (so far; fingers crossed!). And then we tend to make more of them, faster, and—because they are clear—*better*.

Practically speaking, I also need to *schedule* these small steps and little wins. Let's go back to this book as an example. It's been on my mind for a while now, just kind of marinating there; occasionally, I'd look at it on the list of possible future projects and think, "You know, I really should get to that." It wasn't until I sat down, pulled out my calendar, chose a free morning, and put "brainstorm ideas for outline for new book" into a three-hour block that I got around to starting. And it wasn't pretty. It didn't come out in a clear outline. But that wasn't the point. My job was not to create a great outline but to brainstorm ideas for what might one day *become* an outline.

So I sat down with my Ugly Notebook with no pressure or expectation other than to spend three hours writing down ideas and thoughts that might one day become part of this book. And I'm writing Chapter 11 now because on my calendar, for the three-hour block I set aside for this morning, it doesn't say, "Finish the damn book!" It says, "Write a crappy draft of Chapter 11."

I can't handle the kind of pressure that "finish the damn book" would put me under; it's too big. Hell, even writing the eleventh chapter seems a little overwhelming. "Write something great" almost guarantees that I'll write garbage or—more likely—nothing at all. But I can write a crappy first draft. You want crap, here it comes! And more often than not, what comes out isn't half bad. It starts ugly, sure enough, but it finds its feet, and in a few weeks, my calendar entry will be "Edit Chapter 11," and my job will then be to polish things up. And I can probably do that in three

BEING
OVERWHELMED
AT THE THOUGHT OF
EVEN TRYING,
OR NOT KNOWING
WHERE TO BEGIN,
IS ENEMY
NUMBER
ONE.

hours, too.

Why three hours? Because that's what it takes for me to get moving, to clear the cobwebs, to shut my internet browser, turn the phone off, and find something as close to flow as possible. And because I know that when I finish the third hour, my brain will be mushy and incapable of much more than letting my body go on autopilot for a while. So that's when I go swimming or eat lunch or move on to something that takes less out of me. I know that three hours on the calendar means two hours of actual getting-shit-done, and that's about what I need. You might need more or less. Your constraints might be different than mine. What matters is that you find them, use them, and work within them.

As I write this, the mornings on my calendar for the next month are spoken for in three-hour blocks to get the rough draft of this book done—the rough draft that no one will see. No pressure and no obligation to make it more than an ugly first effort. But each day, my job (at least where this project is concerned) is clearly defined in small, very manageable steps.

Tomorrow, I'll sit down and work on what might be a really bad draft of Chapter 12. I can do that. This approach has worked well for me on other things as well—bite-sized pieces on the calendar. "Go to the pool and do ten laps" is easy and usually results in me swimming 50. Because I get momentum by easing into it so when I've done ten laps, I think, "Well, I came all this way and I'm wearing my red swim trunks and they're faster than the blue ones, so I might as well do ten more." And if I'm on a roll when I'm writing and three hours turns into four and I eat lunch a little late, well that's OK. The hard part isn't stopping; it's starting.

Tactically speaking, my To-Do List is nothing more than a bunch of ideas for things I really probably ought to get done someday. Some of them are more vital than others. But the important ones don't get done until they get broken down into small, clear, manageable wins, and put on my calendar so I'm not left thinking paralyzing thoughts like, "What should I do today?" or "When should I start the next project?" The decision was already made. It's on the calendar, and it's small enough that it's easier just to get it done than to put it off.

It's all an evolution. It begins in my Ugly Notebook, moves as a larger item to my To-Do List (which should probably at this point be called my Do This Eventually List, but I'm practicing brevity), and eventually gets broken up into smaller, easier pieces, on my calendar. And because I like ticking the little boxes, I'll sometimes move it back to a "just for today" list. Today, as I write this in real time, my calendar tells me to write Chapter 11. But my little list just for today does, too. It also tells me to go ride my bike at 11 a.m., answer email for an hour after lunch, and be ready for a phone call at 4:30 p.m. That's my day. Plenty of other stuff will fill in the empty space, but that little list gives me a chance to make some checkmarks, and I'm just weird enough to find that motivating.

If starting is as hard and unnatural for you as it is for me, it could be that you're not breaking things into pieces small enough to chew. Being overwhelmed at the thought of even trying, or not knowing where to begin, is enemy number one. For most people, procrastination is not a thing we do so much as the simple not doing of the things we would do otherwise if they were clearer, smaller, or less intimidating. Try stacking the deck in your favour by making them so. Break it down until it is small enough and clear enough, and give yourself a chance for the small wins that, over time, accumulate into something great. Or they might, but don't put too much pressure on it, or on yourself. For now, just start in little pieces and let them be as ugly as they need to be. One step at a time until you can tick the box.

Ugly draft of Chapter 11? Tick. I'll clean it up later, but it's done. Two hours ago, there was nothing here but a blank page. That's how things get done. As long as we don't get distracted.

12
DISTRACTED!

Much has been written about the astonishing power of social media to distract us and fragment our focus. Not one to leave a (metaphorical) dead horse unbeaten, I'm going to add my voice to the fray. Again. If this book is a discussion of everyday creativity, getting more done, and overcoming the obstacles to starting those same things, then distraction has to be among the most pernicious of those obstacles.

Creativity of any stripe requires our undivided attention. If we are to get to flow, that state of focus in which we accomplish our best work unhindered, then we have to concentrate and to do that, we need to be present. Have you ever had a conversation with a friend who keeps checking their phone as text messages come in? They pick it up, read the message, fire off a reply, then come back to you as if nothing had happened, sometimes muttering a distracted apology. It's like they're there and then suddenly—poof!— they're gone, ducking out of the conversation, leaving you hanging. And when they do come back to you, the conversation just isn't the same. "Where were we? Oh right, we were talking about—PING!" The sound of the reply to the reply chimes in, and the conversation is once again derailed. How deep do those conversations get? How much effort does it take to start again and again and again?

The human brain is an astonishing thing, but still not so capable that it can do more than one thing—especially one new thing—at once. If you're doing something you've done a million times, like reciting a poem you've had memorized since childhood, you might also be able to ride a unicycle and juggle kittens and never miss a beat. Or a kitten. But that's not what you're doing when you're making new things: writing a speech, creating the marketing campaign for a new product, or creating that new series of chainsaw carvings.

Making new things, or engaging in any part of the creative process that matters, requires a level of focus that frowns on half-brained measures. But many of us are still convinced that the idea of multitasking has more merit to it than the idea of a flat Earth, and the science doesn't seem to back that up. One study I found from the University of London implies that people who multitask during cognitive tasks experienced a drop in IQ of 15 points, leaving them on par with an eight-year old child. Do a quick Google search for "studies on multitasking" and you'll find a wealth of studies and commentaries on studies that over and over again show that our brains don't do more than one thing at once very well. It's unproductive, wastes time, and yields poorer results.

And yet, people continue to text and drive. Maybe not literally; I would hope we're all smarter than that, but metaphorically. We sit down to do our work and notifications constantly ping for our attention. We dive in and out of what should take an hour or two of our attention to "just check in" on social media or the news or our emails or to talk to a co-worker. And each time we do that, we experience a loss of focus and flow. Remember flow? Flow requires focus. When we lose it or give it away, the momentum disappears, and what should have taken an hour not only takes twice that, but the result is poorer for it.

The alternative to multitasking (because there is no less to accomplish in your day) is focus-stacking: to do one thing at a time with extreme focus and then another. This is not an easy sell, but it's necessary. If distraction is one of the reasons we don't start projects or that the efforts to begin yield less initial fruit and therefore take longer to get off the ground, then we need tactics that allow us to cope and re-jig the whole thing.

Email doesn't have to be a distraction. Nor does social media. Or your spouse or co-worker. A distraction is only a distraction when it pulls your attention from what you are doing. But if you give yourself an hour to do that thing, shut down notifications, close the door to your studio or office, and subsequent to that hour, you schedule 30 minutes for email and social media or a cup of coffee with your partner, you give each task its place and both get done, and done better. This is not necessarily an argument to do less (though you might also give that some thought); rather, it's an argument to do one thing at a time and to be aggressive about shutting out distractions while you focus on the that one thing.

I think we get less done because we're just overwhelmed with it all—and it's easier to spend a day feeling busy and switching focus from this to that and back again—than it is to slow down, take a deep breath, make a plan and take

MAKING
NEW THINGS,
OR ENGAGING IN
ANY PART OF THE
CREATIVE PROCESS
THAT MATTERS,
REQUIRES
A LEVEL OF FOCUS
THAT FROWNS ON
HALF—BRAINED
MEASURES.

things one at a time. It is not enough to put a two-hour block on the calendar to get the thing done, or to make those ugly first efforts. It's got to be *undistracted* time. The ringer on the phone stays *off*. No buzzing, no vibrating: off. Same with email. In fact, put the phone somewhere else or face down. Close the browser. And then do one focused thing at a time.

This isn't sexy. It's not one of those strategies for getting shit done that's going to get anyone really excited or ever go viral. It's not the hero we want (because what we want are shortcuts and "life hacks"), but it is the hero we need.

Focus matters. Focus takes our work to new places; it gives us new ideas and connections, helps us avoid errors, and allows our brains to bring their A-game to what we do. But focus takes time, and that's what multitasking steals from us: the time to go deeper with the thoughts, to stay on track for longer, and to get to flow. The most distracted people I know are the ones who feel they've got the least amount of time. Sure, they're always busy (so busy we can't have an uninterrupted conversation for half an hour), but at the end of the year, have they done more than put out a bunch of little fires or done any of the really big, significant things they wanted to do? Almost certainly not. Always busy, they almost never move the needle on the important stuff.

In his book, *Deep Work*, author Cal Newport makes a distinction between the kind of work that matters to us, the career-defining work, and the stuff that competes for the attention we need to accomplish that deeper work. The paradigm has been helpful to me in distinguishing between important work and urgent work and making specific time for both. Writing this book is important to me; it is not urgent, but it gets my best time. So does my podcast. And my photography. And the urgent stuff, which will always be there no matter how often I tend to it, could forever keep me from doing what's important if I allowed it to. Asking myself every week, "Am I doing my deep work first?" has changed the way I prioritize.

A singer/songwriter could spend so much time tending to the urgent emails and social media that she never gets the album done when it is the album that is most important. An author can be so distracted by other things, none of them trivial, that he never gets around to writing the novel that would otherwise define or establish his career. A coder could spend forever debugging an older project, distracted by the imperfections, that they never make the new, bigger, more important thing that requires their focus.

What kind of work is most important to you? Which things will make the biggest difference in your career or life? And which things are pulling you away from that?

Where people get hung up in answering these questions is in believing that this is a call to choose between the important and the urgent, when life doesn't often give us that luxury. And because life does have this way of happening all at once, we also try to deal with it all at once. But it is not an either/or. It's a when and a how. It is a shift to mindfulness, and a change in thinking from trying to cram it all into our limited time, a little here and a little there, to being sure we do the most important things first.

13
TIME: BIG ROCKS FIRST

Everyday creativity takes time. The things we make don't often happen in the smallest margins of our lives—a little here and a little there. They take blocks of time, and while the size of those blocks will differ for us all, they're still blocks and not slivers. Slivers aren't helpful. Picking away at some project or another for 10 or 20 minutes at a time won't get you into flow and it won't get you past the ugly. We need time, and that's a problem because life has this way of happening without our say-so; with kids, spouses, running a household, maintaining a career and all the other legitimate distractions, you can be forgiven for thinking it's a miracle we get anything done at all. I want to help you find that miracle more often.

Time is a resource. Not only can it be managed better, but if we valued time more, we'd be less flippant about the way we use it. Remember that old adage, "Time is money"? It's rubbish. Time isn't money; it's so, so much more valuable. Money you can borrow, save, and hide under the mattress. Time? Time just keeps moving—you can't store it. That makes it even more important that we discuss this and change our thinking about it.

One of the questions I hear almost weekly from creative people struggling to do their varied things and make art with their lives is this: How do you find the time? Well, you don't *find* time any more than you find money. Leftover time is about as common as leftover money, which is why financial people will tell you to pay yourself first and put X% into savings *first*—before you start spending it—because they know if you wait to save what's leftover, there won't be any. Ever. It just doesn't happen. It is a reliable quirk that unless we pay ourselves first, we will spend what we have, and if we get a raise, our appetites will expand and we'll spend that, too. It's the same with time. It has to be put aside intentionally.

You have got to accept that there are only so many hours in the day. If possible, count the ones available to you. I have no kids. I have no pets. Until recently, I didn't even have houseplants. So I have more hours available to me than you might. That doesn't matter. We're not comparing because you are not me. How many hours do *you* have? Whatever the number, the next question is, do you need more? If the answer is yes, then you've got three options: start trimming, start saving, and stop wasting.

I find trimming the easiest adjustment to make to my time. Every one of us has things we don't need to spend our limited time doing. Some things can simply be cut, like binge-watching TV for three hours in the evening. Cut it to one. You've just freed up two hours of the day. That's a useful block of time.

What about cleaning the house? Right now, we delegate the bi-weekly cleaning of our home and pay someone to do a better job than we could possibly do, in less time, for about $100. Is it worth $100 to free up a couple of hours of your week? Could you do something in those two hours that would make you more than $100 or something that would give you more than $100 worth of pleasure? I guarantee you could. It's the same with our lawn. Our gardener comes twice a month and does a better job than I could, leaving me to do something more productive or creative with those with two hours than being out there and killing all the plants.

You must free your time. Could your kids do the laundry? They need to learn eventually, right? What about the dishes? If you're the cook in the family, what about asking your partner to cook dinner a couple of nights a week so you can gain an extra hour or two? If that terrifies you because you know he'd accidentally poison you all, then be creative. Batch the effort and make twice as much as you need occasionally and freeze half of it so it can be reheated later by anyone in the family. You've got to be ruthless about reclaiming bigger pieces of your week, and being less overwhelmed with it all.

On the same note, look at your day and see where you're losing valuable blocks of time. Forgive me for repeating myself, but you need blocks: not small pieces that are broken up by this and that, a few minutes on social media, followed by replying to the unexpected email that you really need to deal with. If you want more meaningful time, batch the small stuff. Email? Give it 30 minutes at the end of the day and don't think about it again. Same with social media. Turn it off for the rest of the day. No notifications. If it's super important, then check in on it while you're eating lunch (unless you're eating lunch with others).

PICKING AWAY
AT SOME PROJECT
OR ANOTHER FOR
10 OR 20 MINUTES
AT A TIME
WON'T GET YOU
INTO FLOW
AND IT WON'T
GET YOU
PAST
THE UGLY.

Most people get so little done because their available time gets cut up into pieces that are too small to use meaningfully. The concept of batching things has changed the way I work and made me far more productive. I apply it on a daily basis (as well as weekly and even monthly), and it helps in reclaiming larger pieces of my day than I once had—pieces that are now useable blocks because they're not divided up into slivers. Put the slivers together, save some time, and gain some focus for more important things.

Batching works in another way for me: if I need a day to do a particular thing, I do only that thing. If I need a week or a month, I make sure that the largest, uninterrupted chunks of my day during that time are given to that one thing. If I'm working on a book and I need August to do it, I schedule no travel and minimal social calls in August and I get it done; usually, that means one block of three to four hours in the morning, uninterrupted. The rest of the day gets spent doing everything else because life doesn't stop just because I need to make something. But you've got to put the big rocks in first.

Imagine you've got a jar in front of you. Also in front of you is a bowl of sand, a bowl of gravel, and a bowl of larger rocks. Now imagine I ask you to get it all in the jar. You look at the jar and think that there's no way it's all getting in there. You might be right, but there's no way to know until you try. This is a well-known puzzle, so I'll skip ahead to the end. The only way to get everything into the jar is to start with the big rocks first. Get them in there, then add the gravel (which settles in around the larger stones), then pour the sand, which also finds room in the spaces left between the other rocks.

In the classroom, this works every time because after you've portioned out the rocks and sand and gravel, it's a terrible illustration if you get to the end and you still have a bunch of stuff left. Real life works differently. There's just no way to get unlimited stuff into the jar. So we have to choose. The jar is our time. It could be your life, the year ahead, or your day. The rocks, gravel, and grains of sand represent the important things that can only be done with the time you've got. The larger the stone, the more important it is to you.

The lesson is clear: you won't get the important stuff in if you leave it for last. It never happens. Not with money, not with time.

Every day, week, month, or year, consider the big rocks first. No, they don't always fit. Life is like that. But at least you'll know right away. And if the big rocks don't all fit in this month, you can move one of them to next month, but put it in the jar now. Get it on the calendar. Too many people are living this metaphor backwards. They fill their days with the trivial, constantly reacting instead of being proactive, and then getting to the end of the day and realizing the big stuff never got started. The novel is no closer to being started. The clay is getting dried out. That new presentation or project is still just an idea. Drat. Maybe tomorrow.

Figure out what your big rocks are, put them in first, so if you have to say no to anything, it's the small stuff. The email can wait. No one dies wishing they'd cleared their inbox. The same is not true of the novel they wish they had finished (or started), the trip they wish they had taken, the time they wish they'd spent with others. And then, because the big rocks can seem overwhelming and paralyze us and you wouldn't be the first person to set a year aside to write a book that you never got around to starting, break it up into small steps and little wins. Don't leave it in one overwhelming and intimidating big rock for a moment longer than you have to. Break it down into bite-sized pieces, and then just focus on that first small piece. And then the next. Don't worry about making it pretty or perfect. You can refine it later. For now, it's important that you just begin. It is so, so important that you begin.

Not enough time? I don't want to be contrary, but none of us have enough time. But you can make it. You can get ruthless about it by carving it out. Put the big rocks in first, say no (or later) to the other stuff by batching it. Something has to give; don't let it be the things that are most important to you, feed your soul, and give you joy. Don't let it be your most important work.

If the last few pages give you a sense that I am ruthless about time, I am. But that ruthlessness does not come from a desire to cram as much as I can into my days, to trivialize recreation, or to live in slavish obedience to the clock, much as I prefer things to run on time. And it is not an admonition for you to do the same. We will all live our creative lives differently and our time constraints will also be different. What we share is an abundance of those constraints and the need for some breathing room.

The muse is not to be rushed. We need time to clear our thoughts—to not rush through the tasks that are the needed next steps on the path to finishing our best work. Some of us need naps now and then, and to do so while feeling the pressure to skip them or feel guilty when we don't, is counterproductive. Life is not a to-do list to be ticked off, but a series of moments in which to be present, do good work, and find challenge and joy.

My admonition to put the important things first and to be mindful of our limited time is made in hopes that you'll find the freedom that comes from making the choices that are sometimes difficult where time is concerned, to build wider margins into your life—margins you don't just cram with more things but into which you can breathe and find a respite from the hurry and the rush.

A rich inner life is key to a meaningful and productive creative life, and you can't do that in a frenzy or without making intentional decisions about how you use your limited time. I don't know what that means for you, but it probably means you need to find a way to do a little less of the trivial and the urgent and a little more of the important and the needful.

14
THE POWER OF RITUAL AND HABIT

In the daily fight to start (ugly or otherwise), it needs to be confessed right off the top that much of what we do—or desperately need to do—is unappealing. Most of us would rather (as if our preferences have anything to do with it) sit and watch TV with a package of Oreos than put our reluctant ass in the chair and write, or pound through whatever new project is calling to you. When we're in the middle of it and things are flowing, there's just about no better feeling in the world. If only we could just jump straight into that, but we can't. Not often. Lucky for us then that our need to create is strong enough that it keeps pulling us back in, if not because we *want* to then because we *must*. Even when our only thought is that we have no idea where to begin today, dreading coming face-to-face with whatever ugly first efforts we make, wondering if today's the day those efforts will just *stay* ugly.

This is one reason we break things down into the smallest pieces: to create small steps, avoid being overwhelmed, and find little wins. But I'm the first to admit that just because those small steps are bite-sized, it doesn't mean they taste good. Look, I love having written a new book. But writing it? Many mornings I'd rather stab myself in the face with a fork. But being an adult means doing things you don't love. When I'm travelling as a photographer, there are days I don't want to get out of bed and walk the streets with my cameras. Tough beans. The alternative is going home no closer to finishing my latest body of work, and that's not an option.

So maybe you have to break things down even further. Maybe your bite-sized piece is just getting out of bed. Maybe it's getting your ass into the chair you write in, or tuning the guitar, or going into the studio. But at some point, you've got to do it.

I think this is one reason so many creative people, writers especially, create routines and rituals. It's discipline, and discipline is not sexy. But after all the mind tricks and the "hacks" and putting the big rocks first, after the Ugly Notebooks and the Small Steps and Little Wins—you've just got to do it. You, and no one else. And it's easier if it's a habit.

If every morning you wake up, put the coffee on, walk the spiral staircase to your office (as I do), and put your ass in the chair and write, *then* you're pulled along by the power of habit or ritual. Half the time, I don't drink my coffee; it goes cold beside me while I write. But the ritual of making it, the smell of it, and those first sips are the same every morning—and they signal my brain that it's time to write, to begin. The same is true when I walk out the door in a new place to make photographs. I throw my satchel over my shoulder, set my cameras to the same settings I always start with, and I open my eyes wide and take that first step.

Much has been written about the routines and rituals of artists and other creative people. Some wear the same outfit every day; some go to the same coffee shop or do a series of repeated actions that signal the beginning of getting to work. No one has more capably written about this than Twyla Tharp in her book, *The Creative Habit*, pointing at one point to sports as an example: *"Athletes know the power of triggering a ritual. A pro golfer may walk along the fairway chatting with his caddie, his playing partner, a friendly official or scorekeeper, but when he stands behind the ball and takes a deep breath, he has signaled to himself it's time to concentrate. A basketball player comes to the free-throw line, touches his socks, his shorts, receives the ball, bounces it exactly three times, and then he is ready to rise and shoot, exactly as he's done a hundred times a day in practice. By making the start of the sequence automatic, they replace doubt and fear with comfort and routine."*

There is something about the repetition of words or actions that triggers our brains and puts things on automatic. Not mindlessly so, but intentionally. With time, this ritual or routine removes the fear and sets into play a sequence of events within which our creativity flourishes because we've removed the burden of deciding when or how we should begin. And if you're not sick to death of hearing about it, that is the hardest part, and anything we can do to increase the odds or stack the deck in our favour is helpful.

Steven Pressfield, author of *The War of Art*, has his own ritual. Each morning, without fail, he steps into his office and starts his day with the Invocation of the Muse from Homer's Odyssey: *O, Divine Poesy, Goddess, daughter of Zeus, sustain for me this song....*

Your ritual (or routine, if you prefer) can be anything, but it must fit. It must work for *you* because that's the only

YOUR RITUAL
CAN BE ANYTHING,
BUT IT MUST FIT.
IT MUST WORK
FOR YOU
BECAUSE THAT'S
THE ONLY THING
THAT
MATTERS.

thing that matters. In the movie *Wonder Boys*, Michael Douglas's character wore the same ratty pink housecoat every day when he sat down to write. It was his armour.

I used to go to the same coffee shop at the same time each day, order the same thing, sit (when I could) in the same corner, listen to the same music (Van Morrison, *Hymns to the Silence*), and that sequence of events set into motion daily writing that led to my first book—and then (because momentum is not to be underestimated) another and another. And here I am, still writing. Although my ritual has changed, my need for the routine and a structure into which I fit comfortably and habitually, without asking questions, has not.

Eleven years after writing my first book, I still begin most days exactly the same way as the day before: coffee, walk up my spiral staircase, turn off my phone and close everything but the program in which I write (Evernote these days), and sit in my chair and think to myself, "OK, let's write some truly awful first words. No pressure; just get the ball rolling". And two or three hours later, I look up and wonder where the time went.

I wouldn't presume to suggest specifically *how* you might incorporate this into your life, only that you do. Give yourself the same advantage of which others have long availed themselves, by making the start automatic and habitual, taking advantage of the way our brain seems to want us travelling on the well-used neural pathways that we establish when we attach our creative efforts to familiar patterns and structure. I don't believe the invocation of the muse is magic, and there's nothing that coffee does for me that tea or a glass of water might not. But it works.

For me, mornings work best, but there was a time in my life when it was evenings with a glass of wine and jazz on the stereo when I did my best work. Now I prefer silence and work for hours without hearing more than birdsong and tree frogs chirping. It's not *what* we do, but *that* we do it—and do it repeatedly to settle our minds and make the starting effort less uncertain, no longer a question but a statement. Not, "Should I begin or where do I begin?" but simply, "I begin."

15
THE POWER OF CONSTRAINTS

Spend any time with creative people and it won't be long before someone starts muttering about "thinking outside the box" as though this is the holy grail of creativity and getting things done. The idea is to escape the assumptions under which we usually operate and to be unconfined by old ideas and paradigms. I'm a fan of thinking outside the box. But when it comes to actually getting started and making something, boxes have been some of the most helpful tools. I might think outside the box, but I do my best work within the limits of it.

If I had to tip my hand, show my cards, and reveal to you my trump card in living a productive and creative life, that card would be the power of constraints. Boxes. There's an idea among wild-haired artistic personalities that art best happens without constraints, but that's consistently shown to be untrue. Creative work doesn't happen best without limits, but within them. Ask anyone who has ever stared down a blank page, any comic who's been told to "just say something funny," or a chief designer told to create an ad campaign with no further parameters. It's painful, and because it provides no starting point (nor any hints about the limits of the project or any specific direction), the possibilities are so endless they only result in paralysis.

Imagine being told you have to give a presentation tomorrow morning. Set aside the immediate fear of standing in front of others; the hardest part will be the very non-specific nature of the request. A presentation about what? For how long? You could spend the whole night just trying to figure those pieces out, never mind getting rolling on the actual project. I feel the same way when I arrive at a new city to photograph, or when I decide to create a new course or write a new book. In the same way that I've already encouraged you to break these big rocks into smaller pieces once you've identified them and made them a priority, I want to suggest you identify or create constraints as soon as possible. Putting it into a box makes it manageable and defines the areas you don't have to give mental energy to, allowing you to focus on the areas that matter.

Returning to the hypothetical presentation, I can only tell you what I do. As quickly as possible, I get decisive and pick a subject and a direction within that subject. In other words, my subject might be photography, but the point of view I will take is more specific. For example, "10 Ways to Make Better Photographs with Your iPhone." Immediately, my options have shrunk from nearly infinite to something I can wrap my mind around.

Then I get out my Ugly Notebook and start scribbling ideas. Possibilities. Not a finished outline, just ideas. My first job is just to make a list of 10. Then I open Keynote or Powerpoint and create a presentation with 30 blank slides. Why 30? It's just a constraint I've chosen, but in this case, it's three slides for each point. And I put my main points on ten of those slides, with two slides in between each point, where I'll place a photograph on each slide to illustrate. Which photographs? I don't know yet, but that doesn't matter.

What I'm doing is creating a constantly tightening structure. Is it limiting? Is it binding? No, it's tremendously freeing. But what if I want 12 points and not ten? What if I want nine? Great! The constraints are there to serve you, to get you started and rolling with as much direction as possible. When you get to the point that you realize you need three images and not two for each point, or that the third point isn't working for you, you're on your way enough that you can loosen the constraints.

I do this when I photograph, deciding on a theme or an idea as quickly as I can, and that's my first constraint. In India, I'm pursuing two different themes in my work: one is specific to expressions of faith, and one is about the ubiquitous auto rickshaws that transport people and goods here and there. But I also limit myself to one or two lenses and to making photographs that are only black and white and horizontal in orientation.

Does it limit me? Not really. I'm free to photograph other things in other ways should I chose to, but for this project, these constraints help me decide where I'll look for the best opportunities. They also eliminate the tyranny of choices that would require me to choose from too many options when I should instead be directing my attention to my choice of moment, what I do with the light, and how I compose the image. Constraints create freedom, and the sooner I recognize or create them, the sooner I can get going on the work that really matters.

Constraints come in as many different ways as there are possibilities in your work, but the principle, as best as it has faithfully revealed itself to me over the years, is this: the sooner you can get to the fewest and most important choices you can, the better. Let's go back one more time to the theoretical presentation.

I already know that the most important part of this is that I have something valuable to say, that I understand the material and care about it, and that I present it well. That's where I need to put my energies. Not in choosing a font or colour scheme (pick one and go with it). The sooner I pick the latter and eliminate the need to make decisions about it, the sooner I can focus on what matters. The actual making of the thing. The ordering of the ideas, the choosing of examples, the wording on the slides. The sooner I can make the most amount of decisions and call them done, the sooner my brain can wrap itself around the big picture and get started. And yes, if you get to the end and you've got time to fiddle with fonts, go for it. But don't spend your limited decision-making resources on the small stuff.

That's where this is all coming from. Making decisions and focusing on the many choices involved in creating something draw from a pool of mental resources that is not unlimited, and overtaxing that pool of resources leads to decision fatigue. If you spend time deliberating over the small stuff, you'll have nothing left for the decisions that actually matter. When deliberately chosen and quickly embraced, constraints return those resources to you for better use, which is valuable all on its own, but when you add that

IF YOU
SPEND TIME
DELIBERATING
OVER THE
SMALL STUFF,
YOU'LL HAVE
NOTHING LEFT
FOR THE DECISIONS
THAT
ACTUALLY
MATTER.

value to the value gained from starting sooner and faster, without the paralysis of choosing between options or starting points, the gain is immeasurable.

When I begin writing a book, the faster I can get started on an outline (my big constraint), the faster I can get to the heart of the thing and find flow and momentum. And within that flow and momentum, I might very well find that my constraints need adjustment: that my outline needs to be changed to accommodate new ideas or whatever changes arise (as they will in any project) once the whole thing gets moving. When that happens, I change the constraints. Having already accomplished their job, I can let the project change organically. That's how these things work; there is always an evolution. But when things jam up on me again, I go back to the constraints or look for ways in which new constraints might serve me better.

To tie into the conversation about big rocks first and the careful use of time, one of my best constraints is deadlines. If getting started is the hard part for most creative people, then knowing when to stop might come a close second. I use the constraint of a carefully chosen deadline.

In writing this book, I scheduled a very specific deadline for the rough draft to be complete. I put it on the calendar and then, working backward, assign one chapter to each day or two of writing, working back to the day I began. Then I add a few days for the inevitability of life getting in the way or things going off the rails, but then I stick to it and keep it tight.

We have a tendency to fill whatever time we give to a

task. If I gave myself a year to write this book, it would take a year. But if I completely lost my mind or discovered an opportunity that demanded I have it done in five days, I would do it in five days. It might not be the same book delivered after five days as it would be in a year, but I'd be surprised if it was really that different. Importantly, the book would be done, and it would be the constraint of a strict deadline that would help me get there. I have never missed a deadline. Actually, that's not true. I missed the last one by about three months, but only because I finished it sooner than I expected and delivered the manuscript 12 weeks early.

I acknowledge that I am better with time management than others (one of my wife's nicknames for me is "The Clock"), but I don't think that makes deadlines any less important to me. And if you struggle with time, it probably makes them *more* important for you. Deadlines help relieve the pressure (though not too much; pressure can be used well to keep momentum), help me establish a working rhythm, and inform when I must start and when I must hit key milestones. If you can give yourself over to their control—to focus on doing the work—you might just find that constraint helps you. If you need a little motivation, make yourself accountable to someone to hit those milestones or promise yourself a reward if you hit them (a reward that is only released to you by someone else).

There is another advantage to looking at constraints through a positive lens. Constraints are inevitable. Everything you ever make or do will be subject to them, and anyone who is used to working with limitations, self-imposed or otherwise, will be better equipped to work with constraints as collaborators and not adversaries when they show up uninvited.

Creativity is really just problem-solving and the seeking of possibilities among challenges, so the sooner you learn to recognize them and play within the boundaries they set, the sooner you'll be able to focus on doing your work instead of fighting the constraints, and the sooner your focus can be directed to the creative efforts you, until now, have assumed limited or prevented by those constraints.

It's true that there are times when we need to direct our energies to remove certain obstacles and constraints. It's also true that life and work and creative efforts will be easier—and sometimes move from being patently impossible to being full of potential—when the challenges are simply eliminated. For most of us, though, those situations are fewer than we think. Learning to work with constraints means adopting a new way of thinking about obstacles and redirecting our focus in ways only constraints can provide. If you recognize legitimate obstacles, then you define the problem and are closer to finding a solution. That's still a win. But if you instead find that those obstacles can be helpful ways to focus your efforts and give structure to your work, then you'll have that much more energy and attention left over to give to the real work of making and doing.

How you apply this idea in your creative work will be defined by your own needs and personality and the context of your work, but the sooner you establish and embrace your constraints, the sooner you will free your mental re-sources for better use, and the sooner you'll start, having relieved yourself of some of the most common reasons and excuses for procrastinating or delaying that start. It's still going to be ugly. Let it be as ugly as it needs to be, but get moving.

16
TRUST THE PROCESS?

Staring at my outline for this book, a chapter on trusting the process in the second half of the book (the half that is supposed to be practical and actionable) seems a little misplaced. But I've learned that trust is active, not passive. It's either something we act on or it's nothing, and if you don't actively trust that our ugly beginnings will become something more—that they are guided by a very real process of refinement—it's going to be very hard to go all-in with our efforts.

The making of anything (and every aspect of everyday creativity) is an evolutionary progression, and it would be very easy to get frustrated and discouraged if you didn't understand that, embrace it fully, and throw yourself wildly into it. It's one of the experiences I love most about creativity; the blind diving into the unknown, waking up and asking myself, "What will I make today?" with no real idea what the answer is. Because I never know. I don't know what this chapter is going to say by the time I finish it. Not a clue. I've pointed my compass in a direction and I'm walking toward it, but I don't know what I'm going to bump into or the detours and discoveries I'll make along the way. I know my brain is going to surprise me, and that's exhilarating to me. But it would be terrifying if I didn't know that at some point, all that bumping around was leading me somewhere.

It is easy to say "trust the process," but in doing so as often as I have (mostly to myself as a comforting mantra to calm me when the so-called process feels more like a dead-end), it sometimes loses its meaning. Say the word "process" over and over again, and the word eventually loses meaning, and you have no idea what you're talking about. So let me try a different word, a less lofty idea that's closer to the whole ugly premise of this book: mutation.

Mutation in the natural world is an error. It's a mistake or a misstep in the natural order of things, genetically speaking. Evolution, which depends on mutations in individuals, is not the story of everything going right and according to plan, but the story of mistakes that eventually lead to larger changes. It's a gross oversimplification, but over time, the positive changes stick because they work, and the negative changes just end up in the rubbish bin. But it all begins with the mutations. Without a gradual accumulation of so-called mistakes, nothing evolves or moves forward.

This matters because while I might not be the most optimistic guy in the world (and it might be a stretch for my imagination to believe that I'm going to get things right more often than not), it takes no mental effort at all to believe I consistently screw up. And if those missteps result in the mutations and errors that will propel my work forward, then believing I've got a shot at making things that eventually work and do what I want them to do isn't that hard. Remembering and trusting this makes it a whole lot easier to sit down and write or take the first blind steps in making a new product, new website, or marketing campaign. It has

WITHOUT A GRADUAL ACCUMULATION OF SO—CALLED MISTAKES, NOTHING EVOLVES OR MOVES FORWARD.

never been hard for me to trust that I will make mistakes that consistently provide new directions and raw materials, and that disarms the fear enough to get my ass into this chair or out the door with the camera, every day, and to start ugly.

The key is being brave enough to be willing to make the mistakes in the first place, and then to recognize which ones fit and which ones to set aside or discard. Remember, this is not a passive process. The mistakes themselves aren't going to lead anywhere promising. But seeing their potential and not being afraid to play with them, and seeing them all as raw materials that aren't to be feared but to be used, is what gets you to the next iteration: playful exploration of the mistakes.

That's what makes it possible to trust the process: not optimism or the belief that the muses have got your back, but the knowledge that mistakes are not only inevitable but helpful and, at least where your creativity is concerned, nothing to be feared.

Your fear of making mistakes will always be a greater barrier to everyday creativity than the mistakes themselves might be. This is why you must not wait until you've got it all figured out before you begin whatever thing you make or do. This is why improvisation is so important and why our fears and desire for perfection serve us so poorly; they postpone or forever block the making of the mistakes that lead to the best of our work. And this is why so-called failure will always be our most faithful teacher and guide, as long as we keep our eyes open and our minds awake to its possibilities.

"But I might make a mistake."

"I have no idea where this is leading."

"What if I start the wrong way?"

You can address these concerns in one of two ways. The first is with paralysis and inertia, and you already know where that leads: nowhere. You won't fail, but you won't succeed. The second is with the understanding that this is how anything good *always* begins; the sooner you begin making those mistakes, the sooner they'll lead you in right direction and give you the momentum you need to carry you through the refinements and the iterations that get you somewhere unexpected and better than you could have imagined. In that way, you don't even have to trust the process. You just have to get out of the way and start ugly.

17
THE POWER OF FAILURE

Over the years, I've become remarkably good at failing; my list of failures is long. I wish I could attribute this to some noble character trait that has me rushing headlong into failure, fears be damned, but I can't. I slide reluctantly into my failures the same way others do, usually while flailing around and trying to avoid the inevitable. But the benefit of so much trial and error in my life has been the discovery that the best antidote to an all-consuming fear of failure is the repeated experience of failure itself. In other words, the more we fail, the less we fear that it will harm us. With every failure, the evidence stacks up in our favour: evidence that suggests our creative failures not only do not harm us, but help us, making us more resilient, more able to recover from (and make something with) those missteps and so-called mistakes.

My failures have been my most faithful teacher, and foremost among the lessons I have learned—and continue to learn—is that I am incredibly resilient. So far, in almost 50 years of living, there has been nothing from which I have not bounced back. There will one day be the final thing that I do not recover from, but I am certain that one thing will have nothing to do with my creative life. You are more resilient than you know, and your failures will prove it to you.

It's unlikely in the extreme that what finally takes you

or me out is a failure made while taking some risk in what we make or create. We will not die or truly suffer harm from boldly putting our work out there or trying some new endeavour for which we feel barely prepared. If anything, we'll trip and stumble, scratch up our knees, and learn something that will be important when we try again. And again.

Failure is inevitable and is the only means by which we really grow and learn. Failure is the mutation that slips un-invited into our efforts, and while I'd like very much for that not to happen, I'd also like a unicorn. Unlike the unicorn, failure is real, even inevitable, and has the power to redirect your efforts or reveal some crucial piece of the puzzle that you didn't have before.

Nietzsche said what doesn't kill us makes us stronger; I say it gives us something to blog about. It's a gift. It's the nudge we need to evolve and bring our work forward with us. And the more it happens, the more familiar we get with it, the less we fear it because we fear what we do not know and what harms us. Creative risk and subsequent failure have never harmed me, though they have hurt at times; hurt and harm are not the same things. And the more I fail and bounce back, the less failure remains a feared un-known. I am confident the same is true of you.

For those for whom there is still so much fear of true harm and the unknown in the creative life, all I can urge you to do is look back. You've made it this far. You're resil-ient enough to have moved forward from whatever bruis-es you've had. You've learned hard lessons. But you're still here. And the biggest lessons you've learned, the ones on which you lean the hardest, were they not learned from risk and the threat of failure, even colossal ones from which you thought you'd never recover? Are you not stronger now in the places that were once broken? Not everyone is; I get that. Life is long, and sometimes the recovery takes all the time we can give it. But on balance, at least where the creative life is concerned, when you look back, do you not see a resilience?

When I look back in search of my most enduring lessons, they came from two painful divorces, a bankruptcy, and a near-fatal accident that forced me to learn to walk again and continues to limit my mobility. Those are the big rocks. In between, there are countless smaller losses and failed attempts, and smaller still, the daily experiments in loving and making and doing that often take a couple of tries to get off the ground. None of them have been anything but faithful to draw me forward into the person I am becoming. That person is the source of all my creative efforts, and so those daily experiments are pulled forward and become richer and deeper, their evolution and mine propelled by the mutations and so-called failures.

The only failure is not getting back up. Giving up. Throwing in the towel and retreating. The failure is only in refusing to learn the lesson because it's the lesson that turns the perceived failure into a positive mutation and keeps the temporary pain from turning into permanent harm. This is more than just looking on the bright side or thinking positively: it's learning. On some level, it is the stubborn refusal

NIETZSCHE
SAID WHAT
DOESN´T KILL US
MAKES US
STRONGER;
I SAY IT GIVES
US SOMETHING
TO BLOG ABOUT.
IT´S A
GIFT.

to let these chances go to waste and slip into our past un-redeemed, without first being stripped of the opportunities and the raw materials they offer us.

My earlier quip about finding something to blog about in the things that do not kill us wasn't written flippantly or insincerely; for the creative person, these things can become the source of powerful poetry, song, visual art, dance, movies, and every other kind of storytelling that we create and put out into the world to embolden it and give it courage to bounce back and learn from the same. It is the lessons from these failures—and the sometimes long walk back from them—that makes us better partners, lovers, friends, parents, artists, and human beings. They become a gold mine of deeper material and the means by which we become better skilled at working those materials.

When we see stop seeing ugly starts (or ugliness at any point in the process) as failure, and we stop seeing failure as a dead-end or the proof that we can't do this and probably shouldn't have tried, rather than the possibility it represents, we become freer in our efforts to make and to do whatever it is we make and do. But more than that, when we choose to do so, we begin to find in those diverted efforts and so-called failures a source of strength and wisdom and the growing seeds of courage.

Your ugly start isn't failure; it's a promise—as long as you don't abandon it but do the work and see where it leads.

18
THE PROBLEM OF BOREDOM

Some of the worst days in my creative life find me wandering the house aimlessly, in a funk, creating nothing, doing nothing, and muttering to anyone who will listen, "I'm bored." This is not only a problem for those listening (though it's a small audience of one and she usually puts her headphones on and drowns out my whining), it's also a problem for me. Not only do I make a living from my creative efforts and need to keep working to keep the lights on, but I also make my life that way, so I'm miserable when I'm bored. That melancholy keeps me from starting new work, becoming an unhappy and unproductive cycle; boredom leads to unproductive days which leads to more boredom, and down I spiral.

Before I go on to tell you how I fight my own boredom and turn the spiral around, it probably helps to know that boredom is not always a bad thing. I don't think being busy all the time is necessarily valuable. In fact, the next chapter deals with the problem of burnout, a problem that often arises because we refuse to slow down and get a little bored. Boredom is a place in the bottom of the up-and-down cycle of creativity to which we inevitably return to give our minds some rest; it's just not a place you want to linger long. I've got more to say about that in Chapter 19, but for now, I'd like to focus on the problem and not the occasional benefits of boredom.

Boredom is a lack of challenge—a mental space in which there is no fascination, no puzzle to solve, and no problem to overcome. It's the inertia of the mind, and it's one of the states of being that is most responsible for the periods in my life when I stall and get nothing done. Sometimes my creative well is just bone dry, and the best response to my boredom is to read a book or otherwise try to fill that well. But other times, because I do have to get my work done, the answer is challenge.

As I write this chapter, I'm into the fourth week of self-isolating in our home, hiding from the world in what are undoubtedly the early days of the Covid-19 pandemic that began in late 2019. This would be a very good time to get bored, to let my momentum slide into stagnation. But by "a very good time," I mean both "the easiest time ever," and "the worst time in terms of my creative health." If I am to keep boredom from destroying my productivity and stealing my joy, I need to embrace or create intentional challenges.

This is really just another way of looking at the principle of constraints explored in Chapter 15. You've got to give yourself a problem to solve and a way to focus your energies. I've given myself six months to create two new books (this being one of them) and two new photography courses. That's a challenge that will keep my mind chewing on problems and testing solutions every day, keeping the boredom at bay most of the time. But there will be days when I find my rhythm on some part of the project for long enough that it stops being a challenge, and when that happens, flow stops. When flow stops, boredom is not far behind.

Boredom is the opposite of flow, and the missing ingredients are challenge and interest. Sometimes you need to set one project aside for a time and focus on something else, to let your interest return. Sometimes you need to begin something else to reintroduce the challenge.

If the only thing I had to captivate and challenge me right now was this one project, I'd grow bored quickly. I can only maintain my interest and my problem-solving in one direction for so long before I need a break. The solution for me is to work on several things at once, all of them at different stages of the process.

Two days ago, I took the afternoon to work on this book—but not to write it. Instead, I worked on the cover designs, stretching a different part of my creativity, a different set of skills, and giving a break to the part of my brain that deals with words and finding a different challenge. This afternoon, I'll work on presentations for one of the courses I'm making. On other days, I might go into my photographic archives for a couple of hours and put together a series of images I can post to social media.

These are tactics that work for me; your approach will depend on what works for you. Some people will work on one thing non-stop until it's done and experience no waning of their interest in the work, nor a loss of the challenge. Some, like me, need more rhythm. I will work on different aspects of all four of my current projects this week, each in its own time, because that rhythm sustains the interest and the challenge for me.

WHEN
FLOW STOPS,
BOREDOM IS NOT
FAR BEHIND.
BOREDOM IS
THE OPPOSITE
OF FLOW,
AND THE
MISSING INGREDIENTS
ARE CHALLENGE
AND INTEREST.

I don't know many creative people who are happy or do their best work, when it no longer fascinates them, or when the work becomes so easy there is no need for the flow that so many of us rely on. For most of us, when the challenge fades, we get bored and no longer engage in the work in the way it needs us to show up. Sure, you can mail it in; most of us have enough skill in our craft to just do the minimum. But that's not the effort that results in something into which we pour our souls or find ourselves. For that, we need challenge to draw out the very best of us. And because it's challenging, uncharted territory that's new and unfamiliar, the only way to begin is going to be a little ugly. The ugly is an indication of the challenge; it's a sign that what you're embarking on is hard enough to tease out the best of you and make you better. The ugly is a promise of the potential of flow.

I can't begin to imagine how this will be specifically applicable to you in the craft or art you pursue. But you do. You know what interests you. You know what challenges your current skill or other aspects of your creative life. The hard part might not be related to skill at all; it might instead be the need to be more vulnerable in your work and to stop playing it so safe. It might be the need to explore new subjects and ideas, and that's scary when you're so comfortable exploring the same ideas you've been tackling for a while. But listen to that fear—that twinge of nervousness (or pang of terror) when you think of new directions or next steps might just be the sign pointing towards the challenging work you most need to be doing.

For others, the challenge lies in finding new ways to share your work with the world. I talk to a lot of photographers who put great effort into making photographs but for whom the idea of sharing that is terrifying. But that challenge, if they would tackle it, would take their work (and themselves as artists) to new places.

Challenge is not about making things more difficult for yourself just to be a masochist. It's about giving your mind a bigger something to flex itself against and a problem to solve. It's about re-engaging the imagination and asking it to work a little harder so it's thinking about the task at hand with all pistons firing. Challenge is about focus; it's the antidote for boredom. Recognizing boredom and realizing that you're at a pivotal place in the creative rhythm is an opportunity to choose growth and pursue flow. Not recognizing it or allowing yourself to remain in that state of being for longer than the break or rest you need is a step backward into stagnation and procrastination.

Bored? Ask yourself what you can do in your current work to make it more interesting to you. Could you introduce an added element or problem that demands more of your attention, something that reintroduces some of the risk that's been missing? What new skill could you learn or experiment with that pulls you from the familiar and injects the uncertain and makes those reliable first efforts a little bit ugly again? That's the sign that you're back on track.

19
THE PROBLEM OF BURNOUT

As I wrote the last chapter, I realized there's a strong connection between boredom and burnout. They seem like polar opposites, but as I was writing and reflecting on the times I have been well and truly bored, I noticed that the one always followed the other—that boredom was the natural part of my own rhythm that has always come after being extremely productive or, at the extremes, overwhelmed with the work I've been doing.

The rhythm goes like this: start ugly, gain momentum, find my groove, focus deeply, get into flow, and then finish with nothing left in reserve, having burned all the fuel that was available to me. Nothing left. And then in the needed break, after that period of challenge and creative effort, it's not long before my mind—unused to the silence and the rest—starts chomping at the bit or getting hungry and bored.

It's almost always like that, though in different degrees of intensity. Burnout and boredom are the extremes of the natural inflow and outflow of the creative rhythm, and I wonder if they're better anticipated and managed rather than avoided. In my life, this is certainly true. I think a little boredom is helpful for a little while. And I think a little burnout (depending on how we define the idea) is also helpful, though also only for a little while.

Boredom and burnout are both a form of emptiness.

We've discussed the former, but I'd like to make a case for the latter because I think in our efforts to avoid it, we conserve fuel. We keep an eye on the intensity of the flame that fires our work and pace ourselves to make sure there's always a bit left, and I've never found that to be a helpful approach as much as it is miserly and results in work that lacks generosity and the kind of abandon that leads to our best work. I think we need to go all-in on our lives, and that includes, perhaps especially, the creative work that is most important to us. I try to end every day as close to empty as possible as the best guarantee that I've done my best and most important work without holding back.

Where this metaphor goes off the rails is when we do this in our daily lives but do not refill the tank. Long-term and damaging burnout happens when the outflow of our lives outpaces the inflow, and that is what we need to avoid. As is so often the case, the wisdom isn't in one or the other, but in both: not necessarily in balance, but certainly in tension.

The most creative times of my life (and by that, I also mean the most productive), both in ideas and in productivity, have been when I've been intensely working and making and doing, but not to the exclusion of reading and exposing myself to new influences and learning new things—matching my output with my input. When I do the former without the latter, I encounter boredom, and when I do the latter without the former, I burnout. Temporarily, it's not a problem, but long-term, both kinds of hunger and emptiness are the two sides of a coin that leave nothing to offer me for the making of my work.

Emptiness is not always bad. Emptiness means that no residual ideas and expectations have been stored safely for years in case you might need them. It means nothing left in abandoned corners of your brain to mold and rot. It means there is more room for the ideas and the thoughts that are most important and fascinating to you now, and it means plenty of room in there for you to get messy moving them around instead of bumping into old stock and empty boxes. This is what it means to have a healthy and vital inner life and to feed and challenge the imagination. Hunger makes you sit down and eat a great meal, to refill on calories and nutrients. The problem isn't becoming hungry; it's when you don't refill enough on the right sources of those calories. You can eat and eat and still be malnourished.

You get where I'm going with this? Can I drop the metaphor now? Only you know if endlessly scrolling through Instagram or binge-watching Netflix or YouTube is filling you with the best kinds of raw materials.

Only you know if, once you've burned through your fuel, you're still trying to keep going on fumes, wondering why the work is both uninspired and uninspiring.

Only you know when it's time to feed the hunger. Shit. I came back to the metaphor, didn't I? Sorry about that. But this is a very real problem for the creative because it comes back to our ability to start and sustain our creative work, and if I have to beat another dodgy metaphor to death to convince you to eat well, creatively speaking, I will.

If you're having a hard time starting, whether that's the

ONLY
YOU KNOW IF,
ONCE YOU'VE
BURNED THROUGH
YOUR FUEL,
YOU'RE STILL TRYING
TO KEEP GOING ON FUMES,
WONDERING WHY
THE WORK IS BOTH
UNINSPIRED
AND
UNINSPIRING.

very beginning of a new thing or you're restarting in the middle of something you've been doing a while, it's worth asking whether you're empty. It might be from burnout; it might be from boredom. Either way, you've got to restart the cycle of fueling great output with great input. Both need to be challenging.

That's my complaint with so much (though not all) social media. It's not challenging; it's fluff. It doesn't push us; it coddles us. And it's OK to be coddled now and then, but as a steady source of influence, it might be no wonder we're not feeling nudged to do more than what comes easy to us.

It's not just social media, either, because there are voices on Facebook, Instagram, and YouTube (to name the dominant platforms as I write this) that will challenge you if you take the time to find them. And the same is true of other media; there are books and film and music and visual arts that will teach you and give you real food for thought, and those that won't. With apologies to Marshall McLuhan, it's not the medium: it's the message. I don't think one medium is necessarily good while another is bad.

I'm getting away from the point, which is that filling the emptiness left by burnout (and of which boredom is so often a symptom) is not about the *quantity* of ideas, but *quality*. Or the ability to find challenges within either, which I have to admit is a possibility if I'm not going to contradict my earlier premise of bad ideas leading to better ideas. However you choose to do it, you've got to refill with the ideas and raw materials that will best challenge you and move you forward and get you starting again.

There is another sense in the idea of burning out, and that's a state of being that won't be helped by reading a book or filling up on ideas. We are physical beings, and our mental and creative activities are connected to our physical well-being in a way that's integral and inseparable. If you don't get enough sleep, drink enough water, or eat enough calories and nutrients (I've now moved on from the metaphor), you'll experience a different kind of burnout: the kind where it's a failure of the engine itself not just a lack of fuel, and that's arguably harder to recover from.

Much as I prefer talking about ideas, the neglect of the body is necessarily also a neglect of the mind, and for these final pages to remain helpful to you it could be the most valuable reminder I can offer is to care for the factory that is the source of all the making and doing you hope to improve by reading this book: your body.

Our creativity is an astonishing process, and you can't lay it all at the feet of the muses. That doesn't make it any less beautiful or mysterious. God knows I have no idea where half the crap I think of comes from or how. But I know that actual physical burnout from lack of sleep or long periods of sustained inactivity or trying to fuel this astonishingly complex machine with a diet of Oreos and whisky would hamper my efforts at everyday creativity in ways that guarantee diminishing returns, poorer focus, and less-skilled execution. My belief that there is a healthy kind of burnout to experience on a regular basis (and even needed for greater sustained creativity) is not the same as the refusal to care for yourself while burning the candle at both ends and muttering, "It's better to burn out than fade away," when others ask if you're OK.

If you can't make the burnout metaphor work for you, abandon it. Take only what's useful. What I'm hoping will stick for you and serve you is the idea of allowing yourself to be generous enough in your creative work that you hold nothing back and regularly get empty enough that you must refill with more and better ideas, more challenging raw materials, and allow as much to flow in as flows out. Our starting points might be ugly, but they do not need to be uninspired or lacking in the kind of fuel and resources we need to sustain these creative efforts. You'll need that momentum because as much as this book is about starting and being unafraid to begin in the ugliest way you need to, the creative effort doesn't end there. It includes refinements, reworking and rewriting, unexpected mashups, and the constant evolution of the rough idea or execution towards those that are progressively more beautiful, and closer to the thing you held in your mind's eye when you started this whole messy thing.

20
BEAUTIFUL ENDINGS

I wrote this book because one of the things I hear from people that I know to be incredibly creative is this: "I wish I were *more* creative." People mean different things by this, but in most of these laments, the sense I get is not a longing for more originality or a way of thinking that's noticeably divergent from the rest of the population, but a desire for it all to be just a little easier, free of risk and the need to leap before the net appears. They want to begin some creative new work, see instant results and call it done, and repeat that pattern until they can look back and see a body of work made over years that just flowed from them like a waterfall in Eden.

We don't want much, do we? Actually, I think we don't want enough. Wanting it to be easy is hoping for work that requires too little of us. It's equating the hard work of everyday creativity with magic, just hoping that if we show up, we'll be a conduit for the muses who require no more of us than that we act as a vessel. And if that's the case, it's not really our work, is it? It's theirs. Well, with the utmost respect for the mystery of the process, I am not a robot on the assembly lines of the muses—and neither are you.

Creativity is a personal process of making things that once were not. It's a process of becoming something you once were not, and it will always cost you something. If you arrive for your daily work, willing to show up and put skin in the game and work through the initial ugliness of new beginnings and the risk of making something that until then did not exist, the rewards are high. You've just got to want them more than the competing desires for comfort and a life without too much challenge. You've got to be willing to go all-in because although it's not a quick process, it is cumulative. And you will one day look back and marvel at all you've created and the way that it maps out the vectors of your own personal growth into the person that art-making always pushes us to become.

One day you'll look back and see each and every one of those ugly beginnings, the ideas that started so tentatively, sketched out in a notebook you hope no one ever sees, but giving them a chance at life: a great big what if? And you'll see the way they became something so different, step by step refined, not despite the mistakes and the mutations, but because of them.

The way you take bad ideas and ugly starts and turn them into something only you could imagine will be different for you than it is for me. Your process has to work for you, so trying to adopt my own approach (itself adapted from so many other sources) and making it yours without knowing your own personality and needs will likely end in disappointment. This book was never meant to be a recipe or a template to wildly increase your productivity or help more consistently you tap into the will of the muses. Mostly I wrote it to help you understand the different facets of one principle that helps me every day to make the things I make and to overcome the most immediate of the many obstacles

NOTHING
YOU CREATE
WILL EVER EMERGE
PERFECT OR COMPLETE,
BUT IT WILL SHOW UP
FULL OF POSSIBILITY
IF YOU'LL JUST
START.

that threaten our work and make all of us, at some point, wish we were "more creative."

When we wish for that increase in creativity, I wonder how many of us do so while looking over our shoulders at others for whom this all seems to come so easily? How do we know to long for an easier creative life if we didn't think it was possible by looking to others who seem to crank out the books or the albums or the new products and marketing campaigns, and wishing we could do that too? We assume it's easy for them. We assume their productivity is a result of some freakish genetic mix-up. I bet they can turn invisible, too. When we compare ourselves to others, we look at visible results from a mostly unseen process and see nothing but beautiful results from beautiful people. No wonder we're left wishing we had what they have.

But we do, in our own way. Creativity is not a talent; it's a work ethic. It's a willingness to start taking it more seriously. I blame the teachers I had. Or maybe it was the system. But while I learned math or science were hard and needed to be learned with homework and study, art was the class for playing—you either had it or you didn't. Not once do I remember getting homework in art class. Or trying very hard, for that matter. We did what we did to the limits of our natural abilities; some did it well, and others learned "they couldn't draw." And we left it at that.

I wish my math teacher had let me off that easily. "Well, David, I guess you're just not good at math, maybe you should just draw me a firetruck instead." You're damn right I can draw a firetruck! Just don't ask me to tell you how fast it's going if two firetrucks both leave different fire halls, ten minutes apart, and one stops for three donuts on the way.

You want to be more creative. I know you do. No one without that desire would read this book just for fun. There's a longing there. However, let's be clear: when we say we wish we were more creative, we're looking for a way around the fact that what we often mean is, I wish I didn't have to work for it.

We always have to work for it, though work is not necessarily the opposite of play. In fact, it's when work and play become separated that I think we step out of flow and our creative efforts slow and become frustrated.

We use the word "play" in our culture as though it serves no serious function, especially among adults. But play is serious business. We learn by playing. That's how we get our start in this world. Play is one of the most creative things we do. Play embraces the Start Ugly mentality because it doesn't feel the need to get things right on the first try, but is open to discovery and dead-ends and U-turns, and doesn't compare its efforts with others.

Our work stops being playful when we begin to focus on the risks more than the rewards. Maybe that's where our joy, once so abundant in the way we made things as kids, heads for the exit: when the stakes feel too high and we begin to strive for perfection.

Starting ugly reverses that. It removes the threat of the imperfect and replaces it with the promise of evolution and eventual refinement. It allows us to take ourselves as playfully as we are serious, and to turn work into play. To be patient with ourselves without also lowering our expectations that the work will become more than it is at the start. To find joy in it again because the pressure isn't so high. Go paint a masterpiece? I don't think so. But go make some truly rough, playful sketches and see if they might contain the hints of something more? I can do that. I can do it every day and never fail. So can you.

When I was a kid, I collected quotes about reaching for the stars and dreaming big and oh so many other exhortations to aim high. Those quotes still inspire me with their wisdom and the longing they call out in me. But they never told me *how*. And the problem with that is when you reach so long for something so good and you never grab hold of it, you become discouraged and eventually assume it's impossible. You begin to do the things that are easy and take on the tasks that require too little of you. You don't stop grasping for the stars; you just settle for the first ones you can reach. So you never grow in the ways that only challenge and mistakes and hard-learned lessons force you to grow.

I wish I'd understood sooner that to dream and accomplish the big and the beautiful, I needed to start small and ugly and refine them from there.

They say beauty is in the eye of the beholder; I think ugly is, too. I think it's a choice. A choice to see possibility and promise within the rough edges. A choice to see every day as a new start, a new chance to embrace the uncertain and the ugly, and to make further choices to follow those somewhere interesting, meaningful, and eventually, filled with beauty.

I wish we could look at our work and any new thing we make in the same way we look at a newborn child, seeing past the very obvious vulnerabilities and the ways in which he or she is not yet an adult, and can't speak or do helpful things that adults do, like drive us to the airport.

No one looks at a baby like that. We look at babies as a beginning and don't burden them with needing to be more than they are, right then, and to do what they have always done in their first days; their only job is to be messy and spit up for a while. To figure out their fingers and make sense of all the new things. And it's the job of the parents not to rush that. To be patient. To not ask their baby to be more than he or she is meant to be, nor to make harsh judgements when the child is not.

Instead, we see babies through a lens of possibility and wonder what they will become in time, and we do our best to help them get there. Of course we do.

But we don't give up on them when they're still in diapers after a couple of days. We don't categorize them as good or bad the moment they make their appearance. And we don't deny them the chance to become so much more than they were when they arrived.

Why do we do that with the things we make—with our ideas and our first efforts?

Why do we burden them, and ourselves, with expectations and demands that will only stop them from becoming the thing they could otherwise one day become? No human being was ever born all grown up.

Nothing you create will ever emerge perfect or complete, but it will show up full of possibility if you'll just start.

Everyday creativity is not a magic thing. It is not the stuff of muses, nor is it a talent you did—or didn't—get. It's making things. Making a poem. Making a business. Making a book. Making a difference or making a change. Whatever it is, it begins with making a start, and much as we all want that thing we make to one day be good, important, needed, valued, beautiful, or whatever you hope it will become, it's going to need time to get there. But first it needs us to start.

The magic, if there is any, is in the beginning.

ABOUT THE AUTHOR

David duChemin is a best-selling author of 32 books, award-winning photographer, and leading expert in the field of creativity. His podcast and book, *A Beautiful Anarchy*, help him share his message with tens of thousands: a rich and fulfilling creative life is for everyone—not just artists.

David spent the last twelve years travelling the world as a humanitarian photographer and creativity workshop instructor on all seven continents. His adventures have taken him through winters in Russia and Mongolia and a summer on the Amazon, as well as months among nomads in the Indian Himalaya and remote Northern Kenya.

Drawing on a previous twelve-year career in comedy, David brings a dynamic and engaging presence as a presenter in workshops, on camera, or on stages for corporations like Apple and Amazon. His expertise has been profiled in magazines and podcasts including *Overland Journal, Elephant Journal* and *The Accidental Creative.*

You can find David at davidduchemin.com, on Instagram as @davidduchemin and on Facebook. His books can be found at CraftandVision.com, Amazon, and at the brick & mortar stores that would be so grateful for your patronage.

FEEL LIKE YOUR CREATIVE LIFE IS A BIT OF A FIGHT? YOU'RE NOT ALONE.

A Beautiful Anarchy is a heart-felt kick-in-the-pants podcast for everyday creators and anyone who's ever mud-wrestled with their muse. These 15-minute episodes are an honest and sensitive exploration of the joys and struggles of the creative life. Let's talk about it.

Listen on iTunes or aBeautifulAnarchy.com